LOST RAI[illegible]YS

OXF[illegible]IRE

Terry Moors

COUNTRYSIDE BOOKS
NEWBURY, BERKSHIRE

First published 2009

COUNTRYSIDE BOOKS
3 Catherine Road
Newbury, Berkshire

To view our complete range of books,
please visit us at
www.countrysidebooks.co.uk

ISBN 978 1 84674 110 4

The cover picture shows Cathedrals Express, No 7026
passing Yarnton Junction and
is from an original painting
by Colin Doggett

Maps supplied by the author
and redrawn by Gelder design and mapping

Produced through MRM Associates Ltd., Reading
Typeset by CJWT Solutions, St Helens
Printed by Cambridge University Press

CONTENTS

ABBREVIATIONS

The following abbreviations have been used in this book:

ATC	Automatic Train Control
B&OR	Birmingham & Oxford Railway
BR	British Railways; later British Rail
BRCo	Buckinghamshire Railway Company
C&PRR	Chinnor & Princes Risborough Railway
C&WRPS	Cholsey & Wallingford Railway Preservation Society
DMU	Diesel multiple unit
DN&SR	Didcot, Newbury & Southampton Railway
EGR	East Gloucestershire Railway
GCR	Great Central Railway
GWR	Great Western Railway
LMS	London, Midland & Scottish Railway
LNER	London & North Eastern Railway
LNWR	London & North Western Railway
LSWR	London & South Western Railway
M&SR	Manchester & Southampton Railway
M&SWJR	Midland & South Western Junction Railway
N&BJR	Northampton & Banbury Junction Railway
OW&WR	Oxford, Worcester & Wolverhampton Railway
ROD	Railway Operating Division
SR	Southern Railway
W&PRR	Watlington & Princes Risborough Railway
WC&PR	Weston, Clevedon & Portishead Railway
WHR	West Highland Railway
WMR	West Midlands Railway
WR	Witney Railway
WRC	Woodstock Railway Company

Introduction

The county of Oxfordshire is situated in the tract of land encircled by the Thames in the south, the Cotswolds to the west, the Chilterns at its eastern border and the Midlands to the north. During the Roman occupation the area was disregarded by and large even though it was strategically placed in the middle of the country and contained some of the region's most valuable agricultural land.

During the 8th century, however, the main settlement of *Oxenaford* (Anglo Saxon for 'ford for oxen') was established and the area began to grow in importance. In the 12th century the county town, Oxford, became the birthplace of its prestigious University.

From the 13th century, Oxfordshire was very much involved in the Cotswolds' wool trade, which brought enormous wealth and prosperity to the region and no doubt provided the financial means for the University to expand and develop into its now familiar collegiate structure.

In 1841 when the Great Western Railway (GWR), under the direction of Isambard Kingdom Brunel, opened its main line all the way between London and Bristol, the station at Didcot lay within the Royal County of Berkshire. It remained so until 1974 when Boundary Commission changes brought that same station into Oxfordshire, together with the towns of Abingdon, Faringdon, Wallingford and Wantage.

Various proposals were made for a railway to link the City of Oxford with this new form of transport but the plans were met with objections from local landowners, the Oxford Canal Company and even the University authorities. Eventually royal approval was achieved on 11th April 1843, and this sanctioned the building of a 9½-mile broad gauge railway from a junction with the main line at Didcot to Folly Bridge, Oxford. Remarkably this line was completed in just 14 months, a feat which would be difficult even with today's technology.

During the 45 years that followed, the main line through Oxford was extended northwards to Birmingham and Wolverhampton, and a number of branch lines were built to provide an important network across the county. Together with several private ironstone railways, they combined to bring additional economic prosperity to the area.

Oxfordshire remained very much an agricultural county but the arrival of the railway provided the means to quickly distribute its produce far and wide and collar the lucrative trade with the London victual merchants.

The GWR became the major railway company throughout Oxfordshire, though it happily co-existed with the London & North Western Railway (LNWR), which built its own Rewley Road terminus alongside the GWR's main line station in Oxford.

There have been many books written on the subject of railways in Oxfordshire, some covering the last days of steam; others have centred on Oxford station and sheds, whereas others have discussed in detail some of the branch lines, which are now lost to the railway scene. This book however, apart from brief excursions into Berkshire, Buckinghamshire and Gloucestershire, concentrates on the area within the county boundary as defined in 1974. Using over 140 photographs, a number of which are previously unpublished, and with the help of outline maps, this volume gives a brief history of the area's railway lines, from pre-grouping days and through the British Railways era, and describes the effects of the Beeching closures, and the railway that has survived to the present day.

The railways in Oxfordshire ran through a landscape of some considerable history and in recognition of this I have included, where appropriate, 'non-railway' references to a particular town or settlement's ancient past.

I have not attempted to produce a 'then and now' book of Oxfordshire's lost lines since there are already such volumes available. However, whilst carrying out recent research, I photographed some of the locations that have significant visible remains and I include a few of these pictures to illustrate the present-day scene.

Lost Railways of Oxfordshire provides information about where the railways were constructed and the towns and villages they served. It should also enable the reader to find what remains of some of these lines and related stations, to walk those that have been preserved, or to enjoy a ride over reclaimed railway trackbeds that have been given a second chance through the efforts of railway preservationists.

Terry Moors

ACKNOWLEDGEMENTS

A book such as this, which recalls some of the past and reveals what is left of the present, requires the assistance of others and, in compiling *Lost Railways of Oxfordshire*, I would like to express my grateful thanks to the following:

Craig Hart of Wantage Museum for searching the museum's archive for period photographs and permission to use them; Audie Baker, Photographic Archivist at Kidderminster Railway Museum, for his assistance in searching and providing me with some marvellous pictures; Roger Carpenter and Rod Blencowe for seeking out a number of excellent photographs from their collections; my friend F.W. 'Tim' Shuttleworth for his encouragement and assistance and the use of some of his photographs; my friend David Thornton for help with locomotive detail and descriptions and for accompanying me on a long trip around Oxfordshire looking for remnants of railways past.

I am also grateful for information, however small, that was willingly provided by Berkshire County Library (Tom); Oxford Local Studies (Cynthia Lewis); Abingdon Museum (Hannah Driscoll); Chipping Norton Library (Miss Howard); Oxfordshire Museum, Woodstock (Cherry Grey); Chris Cavanagh of Young's garage Woodstock, and the Librarians of my local library at Kidsgrove who located a number of out of print books for me; and last but not least, Paula Leigh of Countryside Books who allowed me freedom to select all of the pictures.

1
The Early Years

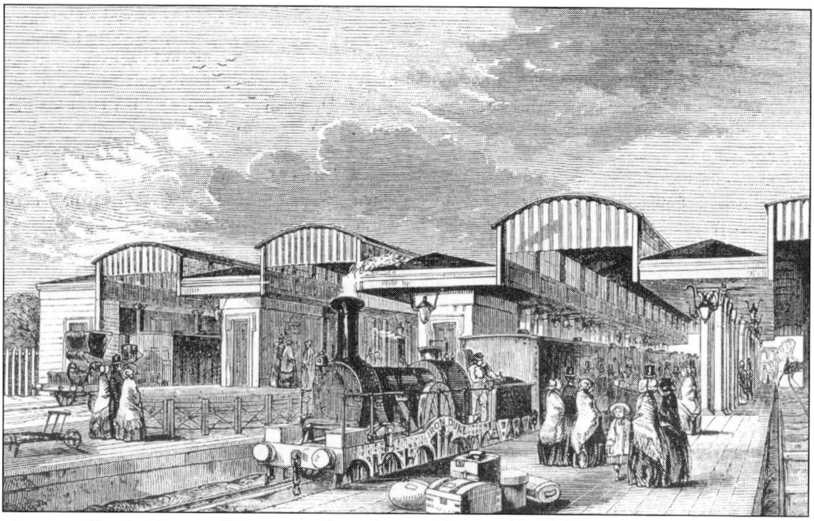

An excellent George Measom drawing of Brunel's Didcot station post-1844, showing a hive of activity on the platforms and its impressive overall roof, which was later lost in a fire, and 4-2-2 locomotive 'Iron Duke' with a train bound for Bristol. (Reading Libraries)

As the Great Western Railway (GWR) produced its prospectus in 1833 for an ambitious broad gauge line, which it proposed to lay between London and Bristol, a branch line to Oxford was also included as a possible connection. But in 1836 as the work proceeded from London to Maidenhead the branch to Oxford had been excluded.

The following year an additional bill was laid before Parliament by the GWR for a line that would connect at a junction with its main line at Didcot and run north to Oxford, ending at a proposed terminus near Magdalen Bridge. The whole idea was met with fierce opposition particularly from the University.

The engineer for the GWR, Isambard Kingdom Brunel, had ambitions beyond Oxford and planned to take his 7 ft 0¼ in gauge (adopted by the GWR directors on 29th October 1835)

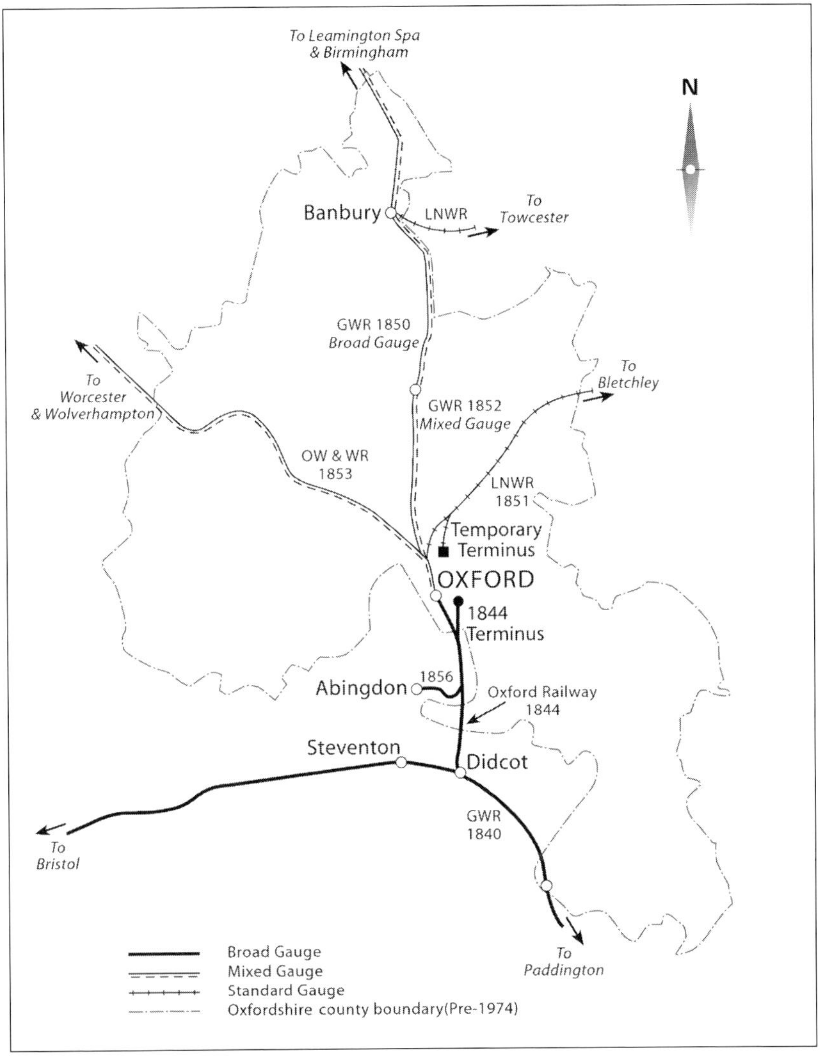

through to the industrial Midlands. In view of this he promptly accommodated the University authorities by changing the original route into the city, together with provision for the terminus station to be situated at Folly Bridge.

These revised plans appeased the University and actually gained their approval, but the railway to Oxford did not proceed since this and two further proposals, submitted by the GWR in

1838 and 1840 respectively, were thrown out because of other determined objectors. These included a number of local landowners and the Oxford Canal Company, which, having constructed over 70 miles of waterway from Coventry to Oxford, was understandably nervous about the prospect of competition from the developing railways.

On the main line, however, construction was running apace and on 30th March 1840 the railway opened to Reading. A few days earlier a local newspaper, the *Reading Mercury*, said, '... this long-wished-for event was expected to attract a large number of spectators and, with propitious weather, a good band, and gay banners, the scene would be highly interesting and enlivening.' As it was, the sun shone brightly for the official opening and from an early hour people from the surrounding area came flocking to the town in order to witness the first train – the 6 am from Paddington hauled by 2-2-2 locomotive, *Fire Fly*, built in 1840 by Jones, Turner & Evans of Newton-le-Willows. This locomotive was one of the Firefly class of engines designed by Daniel Gooch, a 21-year-old engineer appointed by Brunel as his 'Superintendent of Locomotive Engines'. Initially the GWR's locomotives were built under contract but this was to change as the first 'in-house' express passenger engine, 2-2-2 *Great Western* was out-shopped at the GWR's new works at Swindon in April 1846.

Public interest showed no signs of diminishing even a little as the railway pressed on, eventually arriving at Steventon. The *Mercury* newspaper's pages were filled with railway-related reports: 'Oxford, Abingdon and the adjacent towns and villages poured forth their inhabitants in droves; every description of vehicle seemed in requisition on the occasion and multitudes of pedestrians were found on their way to witness the triumphant results of scientific enterprise. So large a concourse of people, we may safely say, has not been brought together in this part of the country for many years as was witnessed at Steventon on Monday last ...'

The first train to travel down the line to Steventon once again carried the GWR's directors and associates, with first class carriages hauled by 2-2-2 locomotive *Charon*, another Firefly class engine, built by Fenton, Murray and Jackson who produced 20 of these locomotives for the GWR. *Charon* was an intriguing choice since it was the name of the mythological 'Ferryman of Hades' who carried the newly deceased across the 'River Styx' that divided the world of the living from that of the dead!

At this time Oxford had more than 70 stagecoach services operating from the town, in every direction, several of which made the 6-hour 'express' journey through to London. As the Paddington–Bristol line opened to Steventon the stagecoach owners took advantage of this by running frequent services from Oxford, via Abingdon, to Steventon station (4 miles west of Didcot), where passengers could catch main line trains.

This profitable arrangement continued for a number of years, during which time the Oxford Railway Company (supported by the GWR) submitted a new proposal (in 1842) for a railway to Oxford and this time the objectors were in the minority. But the University, although making no formal objection, made it known that this increased mobility might affect a student's morals! In order to meet these concerns an agreement was reached with the railway company to limit the availability of train travel to certain 'classes' of student – the finer points of which would be determined by the University.

As a consequence, Parliamentary approval was granted on 11th April 1843 for a line to be built from Didcot to Oxford. The following year, after official examination by railway inspectors, accompanied by Brunel, the line opened to traffic, with the first public passenger train arriving at Oxford's 'Grandpont' station at midday on 14th June 1844. A special train had in fact operated over the line a few days earlier and this consisted of first class carriages occupied by more than 40 VIPs, including Brunel and the GWR's company secretary, Charles Saunders.

Departing from the majestic newly-built station at Didcot, with its grand overall roof, the train took just over an hour to reach Grandpont station, where, ironically, the passengers completed their journey into Oxford by stagecoach.

It is interesting to note that with the dawn of the railway age and the prospect of shorter journey times, stagecoaches continued to operate from Oxford's Mitre and Golden Cross inns until 1890 by which time horsepower could no longer compete with the steam engine and the 'iron road'. It is likely, however, that one of the reasons for the stagecoach's longevity could be the level of passenger comfort that railway carriages offered at that time, with first, second and third class seats provided on most trains.

Culham station, between Oxford and Didcot, was one of the intermediate stations provided on the Oxford Railway. It was a substantial affair, being built to Brunel's design, and when opened in 1844 it was known as Abingdon Road but then renamed Culham in 1856. This picture was taken in 1960 and shows clearly the imposing structure. (Author's Collection)

First class carriages accommodated up to eight passengers and had glass windows and sun blinds. As for the second class coaches, which had a roof but no glazed windows to the sides, the *Illustrated London News* had this to say: 'In cold weather the second class travellers talk but little. They wrap up the minute they get into the train, preparing for the worst, and after a few exchanged courtesies – lending an umbrella to an outsider, or spreading a cloak over two or three pairs of knees – you heard their voices no more.' A coroner's jury once went a step further when it returned a verdict of 'Death from exposure while travelling in a second class carriage on the Great Western Railway!' The third class carriage, as one can imagine, was even worse. They were in fact open trucks with no roof or seats, and usually positioned behind the engine where passengers would be entirely exposed to the weather and be treated to all the smoke and soot ejected from the locomotive! The *Illustrated London News* again reported, 'These rattling pig pens on wheels, misnamed third class carriages, are despicable affairs … a species of horizontal shower bath …'

In spite of this, the railway flourished and following the GWR's inroads into Oxford a succession of major railway schemes followed. For the GWR, Oxford had now become its northern bridgehead and this was to be Brunel's gateway to the Midlands, in direct competition with the London & Birmingham Railway's service from Euston.

On 3rd August 1846 the Birmingham & Oxford Railway (B&OR) was authorised, but from the outset a problem had developed with the B&OR shareholders, where a number were undecided whether or not their shareholding should pass to Euston or to Paddington. In the end, however, the GWR finally reached an agreement and completed its purchase of the B&OR on 31st August 1848.

There were still access problems to be resolved at the Birmingham end of the line but in the meantime the GWR constructed the first section, a broad gauge, 24-mile, single line from Millstream Junction, Oxford to Banbury. The line opened on 2nd September 1850 but required both north and southbound trains to carry out reversing manoeuvres at Millstream Junction in order to gain access to Grandpont terminus station. When the line to Birmingham opened throughout on 1st October 1852, a new station had been constructed more central to Oxford (approximately 1 mile north of Grandpont) which proved to be more convenient to passengers and less costly since they were no longer required to pay bridge tolls (over the river) in order to reach the railway. The old Grandpont station remained open as a goods terminus for another 20 years before it closed completely on 26th November 1872.

Whilst the GWR pressed on northwards a new standard gauge railway was approaching Oxford, namely the Buckinghamshire Railway Co (BRCo). It was constructed in conjunction with the LNWR, with the line coming in from Bletchley, via Verney Junction, at which point another section of the BRCo branched north-west to Banbury. The line from Verney Junction to Banbury opened on 30th March 1850 followed by Verney Junction to Oxford on 20th May 1851. At first, trains to Oxford were required to stop at a temporary 'Oxford Road' terminus, until the line was extended into Oxford – running alongside the GWR's line to a brand new 'Rewley Road' station, built on the site of a 13th-century Cistercian monastery – Rewley Abbey.

A view of Oxford station in 1912, looking north, with a lot of activity on the platforms. What the gentleman is doing straddling the Up line is not recorded! (Lens of Sutton Collection)

Interestingly the station was constructed for the LNWR by Fox, Henderson & Co who, at this time, were the main contractors for London's Crystal Palace, and it is recorded that the company used the same pattern of cast iron supports for the Oxford station building. The following year Rewley Road station would share the site with a new Oxford 'General' station situated on the adjacent GWR main line.

The next line to join Oxford's rapidly increasing railway network was the Oxfordshire, Worcester & Wolverhampton Railway (OW&WR) which, after early problems concerning underestimation of building costs and disagreements with the GWR, finally opened to the public with a standard gauge train (as far as Evesham) on 4th June 1853, and while the line was mixed gauge for the most part, broad gauge trains were never used.

OW&WR trains made the connection with Oxford via a newly constructed Wolvercot Junction, north of the town, and finally running over mixed gauge tracks into the GWR station. At this point the OW&WR trains could continue no further because the line south of Oxford was then broad gauge only. However, this situation changed on 1st April 1854 when OW&WR through services, from Worcester to Euston, were made possible by a new 1½-mile standard gauge 'Yarnton Loop' that connected with the Buckinghamshire Railway at Oxford Road Junction.

During the following years, as the 'railway mania' continued, the GWR gained a foothold in Birmingham and Wolverhampton and a number of branch lines radiating from Oxford's main line were completed. The GWR's premier Paddington–Birmingham service, although challenging the LNWR's route from Euston, was 16¼ miles longer and Oxford was also becoming congested as services increased – a situation that prevailed for many years.

By the end of the 19th century all broad gauge track had been converted to standard gauge and the GWR was looking for ways to compete more effectively with the LNWR. In 1899 the GWR joined forces with the Great Central Railway (GCR) to build a line that would benefit both companies and in particular secure a shorter route between Paddington and Birmingham for the GWR. From High Wycombe the new line ran through Princes Risborough, where the GCR turned east for Aylesbury and the GWR headed north through Ashendon and Bicester to join the Oxford–Birmingham main line at Aynho. The new line opened in 1910 and was known as the 'Bicester Cut-off'; it provided the GWR with a London–Birmingham line of 110½ miles in length –

Running off the shed and onto the Up through road at Oxford in 1930 is 'Badminton' class 4-4-0 No 4116. A new signal gantry replaced the interesting wooden signals in 1959. (S.H.P. Higgins/F.W. Shuttleworth Collection)

Standing outside the LNWR shed at Oxford is ex-Midland Railway 4-4-0 compound No 762. In this undated view it is interesting that the locomotive is attached to an LMS-built tender. (Author's Collection)

2½ miles shorter than the LNWR's route. From then on there was fierce competition between the two companies to provide the fastest trains possible.

Oxford continued as a very busy station and no significant changes took place, other than the two stations coming under joint management in 1933. In 1951 Rewley Road station closed to passengers and all services were transferred to the ex-GWR station. The goods yard remained active right up to 1984, thereafter lying derelict until 1998 when the site was cleared. The station building had achieved Grade II* listed building status but following a controversial planning row, concerning a new development for the University, it was eventually dismantled and relocated to the Buckinghamshire Railway Centre's Quainton Road where, happily, it was rebuilt as a working station, opening in 2002.

The Oxford–Bletchley–Bedford–Cambridge line (nicknamed the 'Varsity Line') became a demanding freight route during the Second World War, as vital material was transported from the Bicester Ordnance Depot via its own internal railway system (which still operates). After the war, passenger receipts, which had been declining for some years, reduced to an unsustainable level and although the line was not recommended for closure in

On 6th June 1933 GWR (ex-ROD) '3000' class 2-8-0 No 3027 (ROD No 1643) at Oxford station with an Up goods train. An ex-GWR coach stands at the platform on the right. (V.R. Webster/Kidderminster Railway Museum)

Waiting at Oxford Rewley Road station on 30th June 1948 is Ivatt LMS 2-6-0 No M3005 with a train for Bletchley. British Railways, as an interim measure, added the 'M' prefix during post-nationalisation renumbering. This engine became class '4MT' No 43005. (F.M. Butterfield/R.K. Blencowe Archive)

Leaving Oxford Rewley Road station is Ivatt LMS 2-6-0 No M3005 with a train for Bletchley on 27th January 1949. In the background is Midland compound 4-4-0 No 41038 shunting tank wagons. (F.M. Butterfield/R.K. Blencowe Archive)

On the last day of passenger services between Bicester and Oxford on 1st January 1968 a two-car DMU waits for the right away for an evening departure to Oxford. (Author's Collection)

A sunny day at Oxford station with what is a tidy and clean frontage, c1964. However, behind the façade the station structure was deteriorating badly and within a year of this picture being taken a decision was made to modernise and rebuild the station. (R.S. Carpenter)

On Sunday 31st August 1952 ex-M&SWJR 2-4-0 No 1335 of Reading shed (81D) stands in the Down bay at the north end of Oxford station with a Stephenson Locomotive Society special for Moreton-in-Marsh and Shipston-on-Stour. The engine, unfortunately, is carrying an unsightly SLS headboard, red lettering on a white background, on the smokebox door. (F.W. Shuttleworth)

On 12th June 1948, '3500' class 2-4-0T No 3562 tops up at the water column in Oxford's north bay platform before its next turn of duty. To the right is an unidentified 'Hall' standing in Cripley Road carriage sidings. (Author's Collection)

A view from the Down platform at Oxford station taken in 1960 as BR 'Standard' class 4MT 4-6-0 No 75022 trundles past the north signal box towards the shed. The signal gantry was installed in 1959, replacing an array of GWR wooden signal posts. (Author's Collection)

Ex-GWR 'Star' class 4-6-0 No 4021 'British Monarch' at Oxford shed on 31st August 1952. The four-wheel metal van next to the tender is Great Western 10T No 85842 in brown livery. (F.W. Shuttleworth)

A view of Oxford Motive Power Depot taken in 1970 with a number of type 4s and type 3 hydraulics waiting their next turn of duty. Steam power had long gone with diesel fuelling racks and washing plant replacing the old wooden GWR steam shed. However, semaphore signals were still in use, giving the illusion that any minute a 'Castle' could steam into view with the Down 'Cathedrals Express'. (Author's Collection)

the Beeching Report it officially closed to passengers on 1st January 1968. The line remained as a freight-only route until 11th May 1987 when an Oxford–Bicester Town service was reinstated by rail operator Network Southeast. The service has survived and is currently operated by First Great Western.

Oxford, then, seems to have fared quite well in retaining its main line railway, not lost in any sense but rather more forsaken as, one-by-one, the various branch lines radiating from the city have disappeared. Services to Birmingham, Reading and London are heavily used, with the Birmingham–Oxford–Reading service, regularly operating with standing loads, which brings considerable criticism from passengers. Extensive freight traffic continues through Oxford and the old OW&WR route is open to passenger traffic to Worcester and Birmingham – served by First Great Western. The line is now singled from Oxford to Ascott-under-Wychwood where double track is regained as far as Moreton-in-Marsh, reverting to single line through to Worcester.

Sadly, Oxford itself provides little tangible evidence for the railway historian. Following various rebuilds of the GWR station structure in 1971 and again in 1990, the removal of Rewley Road station in 1998 and extensive commercial developments, nothing now remains of the original railway architecture.

2
Princes Risborough to Oxford

A general view of Princes Risborough station, looking in the direction of London, with two attractive GWR bracket signals, goods shed and sidings and to the right of the picture the large water tower. The single track leaving the main line at the extreme right is the station avoiding line leading to the Down bay and the lines to Oxford and Watlington. (F.W. Shuttleworth Collection)

At the end of the 17th century, if so inclined, you could have boarded the *Flying Coach* stagecoach service from Oxford and be in London the same day. However, if you lived in Thame, a market town of some repute, a trek to Wheatley would have been necessary to catch the coach, hoping that you reached there without being ambushed by highwaymen!

Thame was also bypassed entirely by the canal builders and even though various schemes were put forward and promises made, nothing ever came of them. As the railways began to appear in the early 1830s the people of Thame were concerned that they might be overlooked yet again. By 1844 Oxford was already connected to this new railway system but it was to be another 10 years before Thame received news that a railway might be heading its way. It was 1st August 1854 when the Wycombe Railway opened its broad gauge line from the GWR's main line at Maidenhead through to High Wycombe and plans were already afoot to extend this as far as Princes Risborough and on to Thame.

During the 19th century Thame had suffered several economic downturns and the arrival of the railway would, none too soon, allow the farmers and traders of the area an opportunity to distribute their produce and materials to more distant markets.

From 1856 plans were drawn up and contractors were invited to submit tender prices for a 14-mile extension from High Wycombe to Princes Risborough and Thame. Parliament approved the scheme in 1857 and two years later, in September 1959, a director of the railway company, Edward Griffin who resided at nearby Towersey Manor, cut the first sod.

The engineer for the line was to have been no lesser man than Brunel himself but he was at that time suffering ill-health and was totally preoccupied with the building of his *Great Eastern* steamship and on 15th September 1859, before the construction of this railway had even begun, he died. Brunel, however, had already made it known that he was about to withdraw from the railway project and recommended to the board of directors a likely successor, an engineer named E.F. Murray. In fact, shortly after Brunel's death, Murray sent a letter to be presented to the directors, extolling his engineering attributes, and although the tone was almost grovelling, they unanimously agreed to his appointment as Engineer of the Line.

Murray did not disappoint them either, making sure that the contractors were kept hard at it, enabling the work to progress quickly. By February 1861 most of the groundwork had advanced as far as Bledlow, where an intermediate station was planned and within three months it reached the site of Towersey Halt and ultimately Thame where the main station was to be built.

Finally, on 1st August 1862, the residents of Thame at last got their railway, when a GWR 'Sun' class 2-2-2 broad gauge locomotive, *Sunbeam*, arrived at Thame station with its three-coach train conveying the company's directors and shareholders.

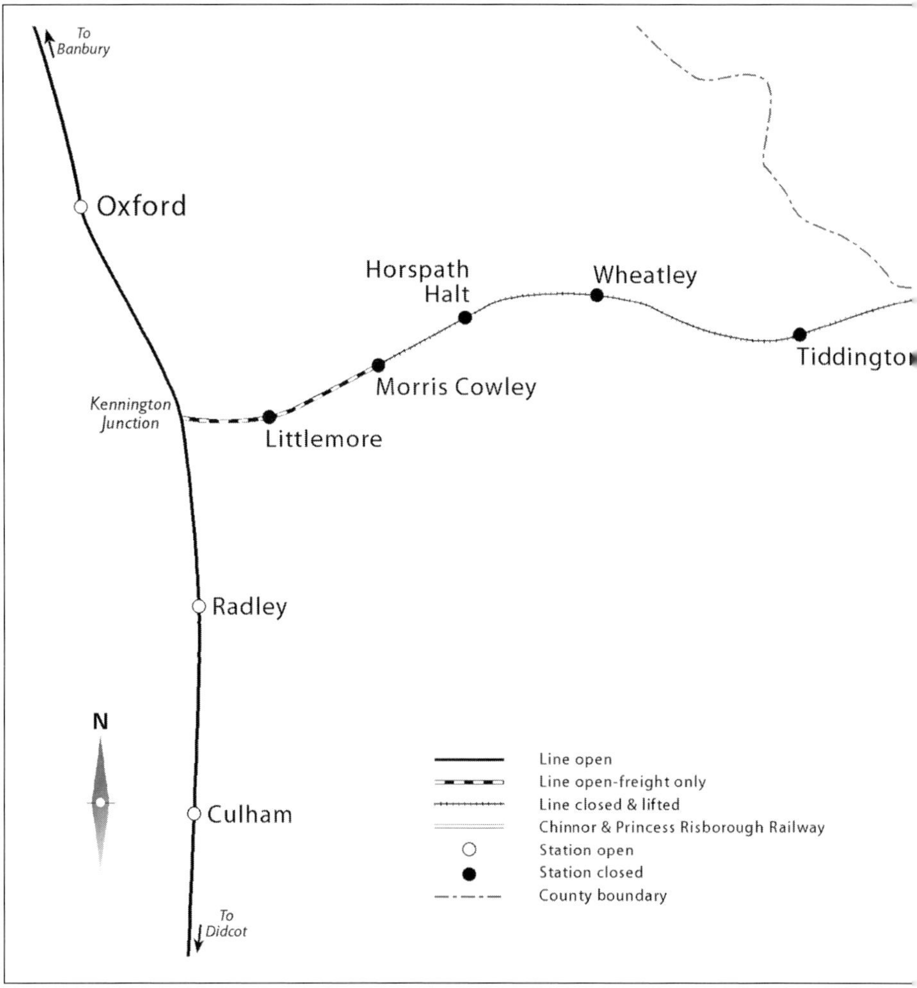

Unusually, there was no official ceremony but a crowd of 500 or so people assembled at the station to witness its arrival.

The next day a regular service to Paddington, via Maidenhead, commenced with an initial timetable consisting of four trains per day in each direction. Although this was a single-track branch line, Thame station was obviously of some importance to the railway as it was built with an impressive overall train shed roof, which was 90 ft long and 46 ft wide.

All that remained now was the push to Oxford albeit in the

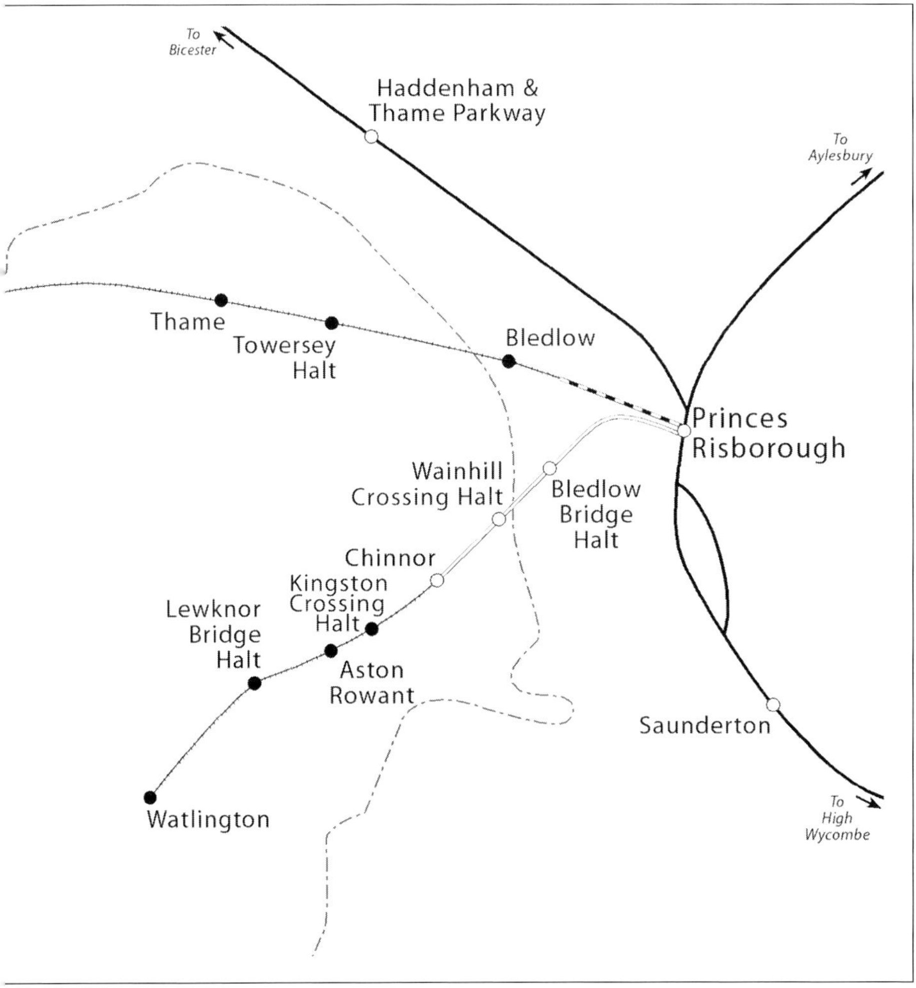

face of vigorous opposition from the West Midland Railway who, a year previously, claimed this would be a threat to their own plans for the London, Buckinghamshire & West Midland Railway for a line to London via Yarnton, Thame, Princes Risborough and Amersham. As it was, the Wycombe Railway was granted authorisation on 28th June 1861 to extend the last 13 miles from Thame to the Oxford main line at Kennington.

Work commenced quickly from Thame, although this final part of the line introduced two major engineering works: a tunnel near Horspath and a 260 ft viaduct over the Thames at Kennington. The tunnel involved an excavation through blue clay, removing more than 640,000 tons of material, followed by brick-lining the entire length of the 1,584 ft tunnel.

As the alignment proceeded towards Oxford vast amounts of ballast were required, most of which was extracted from a gravel pit at Cookham and transported by special train workings.

Members of the clergy obviously took an interest in railways from the early years, judging by the diary of Rev Elton, vicar of Wheatley, who recorded the daily goings-on in and around the railway works. On 9th October 1863 he writes, 'Upwards of 100 men near here. They fetched buckets of spirits on yokes from the "The King and Queen" …'. An interesting notion given today's health and safety culture!

It was anticipated that the line would be completed by the end of June 1864 but in the end it was October before an inspection could be undertaken by the Board of Trade Inspector, Colonel Yolland, who passed the line fit for use.

The opening took place, again without ceremony, on 24th October 1864, providing Thame and its neighbouring villages with travel opportunities to reach Oxford or London and beyond. The initial timetable consisted of four trains per day in each direction (Monday to Saturday) and two on Sundays, all of which were worked by the GWR.

On 1st February 1867 the Wycombe Railway was absorbed by the GWR and three years later the entire line between Kennington Junction and Wycombe Junction, Maidenhead was closed to traffic for gauge conversion. From 23rd August 1870 to 1st September 1870 all broad gauge track was relaid to standard (4′ 8½″) gauge.

Apart from giving the GWR a useful alternative route to Paddington, the line created a steady growth of passenger and freight services, with local passenger trains worked by a number of classes of locomotive, including '517' class 0-4-2T engines, with freight trains in the hands of William Dean's 'Dean Goods' 0-6-0 tender engines.

In April 1908 the GWR allocated four of their steam railmotors to Oxford shed in a bid to increase patronage by calling at the various halts on the line. The weekday timetable provided five services to Oxford, but only three of these covered the whole route, with just two of the four return journeys operating through to Princes Risborough. As in other areas, railmotors were not popular with passengers and as revenue did not meet the GWR's expectations they were withdrawn completely in May 1913.

As the Morris Motor works opened its factory in the 1920s the line took on an important role as a freight route to bring in materials to the factory. With an annual output approaching 20,000 cars, most of these were also shipped out by rail. The Second World War saw further increases in traffic with supplies for the war effort and special hospital trains to Wheatley where casualties were transferred by ambulance to the newly-built military hospital at Holton.

Following the war, the line continued to operate with frequent freight and passenger movements but as the consequences of the Beeching Report were looming and the problems associated with the high cost of maintaining Horspath Tunnel became known the line was recommended for closure. This occurred on 6th January 1963 when a passenger train used the line as a through route for the last time. The section between Horspath and Thame was closed to all traffic in 1965. The section from Princes Risborough to Thame continued as a freight line for oil traffic only until 1989 and Kennington Junction to Morris Cowley ('Mini') works remains open for freight only.

Taking an imaginary trip down the line today, we leave Princes Risborough station from the Oxford/Watlington bay. The line heads westwards on what appears to be double track but it was in fact the Watlington branch line, which ran parallel with the Oxford line for the first half mile, at which point the Watlington line turned sharply south-west. The Oxford line carried straight on for approximately one mile before reaching the first station, Bledlow.

Bledlow, just on the border of Oxfordshire and Buckinghamshire in the charmingly named parish of Bledlow-cum-Saunderton, gets its name from an Anglo Saxon term meaning 'Bledda's burial mound'. Unfortunately for Bledlow folk, the station lay over a mile from the village. The station was a compact affair; situated by a minor road crossing, it had a single platform with a signal box partway on the ramp and a single-track goods yard that handled mostly farm produce. Alongside the signal box was a combined stationmaster's house, a booking office and a waiting room. When first built, the waiting room

A view of Bledlow station c1965 after withdrawal of passenger services. The signal box has been removed and replaced by automatic half barriers. Although the platform is looking a bit ragged the station building is in private ownership with various improvements being carried out. (Author's Collection)

had an open front to the platform but this was subsequently enclosed with an impressive glass panel looking almost like a conservatory!

From Bledlow the line continues for the next 3½ miles over countryside that alternates between level and gently sloping gradients before arriving at the next station, Towersey Halt, which was conveniently situated on an embankment next to the Towersey–Chinnor road, approximately ¼ mile from the village. It was a simple single structure built entirely of sleepers, with timber handrails to the rear of the platform, complete with a GWR-design corrugated iron 'pagoda' shelter.

Towersey Halt was quite a late addition to the line; opening on 5th June 1933, it was in continuous use for the next 30 years, closing on 7th January 1963. Today what remains of the embankment is still visible, together with the bridge that carried the railway over Chinnor Road.

From here the line descends on a shallow 1 in 200 gradient for the ¾ mile run into Thame, passing beneath the B4445 Thame to

Towersey Halt, with its timber built platform and typical GWR 'pagoda' shelter, as it was c1965 after withdrawal of passenger services on 7th January 1963. (F.W. Shuttleworth Collection)

Chinnor road before entering the station. Thame, as described previously, was the largest station on the line, with full passenger facilities, a goods yard and shed, loading dock and a GWR 28-lever signal box.

Thame itself had its origins in Anglo Saxon times with agriculture being its main occupation. In 1640 it took turns sheltering both Royalists and Parliamentarians and as the town prospered in the 18th century the town hosted a visit by the preacher John Wesley. However, because of his radical views the church authorities denied him a sacred venue and the gathering assembled in an upstairs room of a cottage in Upper High Street (now a betting shop) but unfortunately the floor gave way under the weight and the congregation landed in a heap on the ground floor!

Looking at the site now there is little left to suggest a railway station existed there, except for one clue: Station Road survives as a cul-de-sac off Thame Park Road.

After Thame the line continues westward towards Tiddington for another 4 miles of countryside that involved several changes of gradient. These were severe enough to merit a number of line-side notices (illuminated at night), warning 'Change of Gradient'

Thame station in 1962, with its overall train shed roof and ex-GWR 'Prairie' 2-6-2T No 6124 waiting to depart for Oxford. (E.T. Gill/R.K. Blencowe Archive)

Thame station in 1965, two years after passenger services had been withdrawn and the station was taking on a distinct air of dereliction. (F.W. Shuttleworth Collection)

A view of Thame station entrance in 1965 after removal of the overall roof. The railway subsequently used it as offices and stores prior to demolition. (F.W. Shuttleworth Collection)

The oil store, water tower and remains of the water column at Thame station in 1965, all of which were removed soon after this picture was taken. (F.W. Shuttleworth Collection)

'5600' class 0-6-2T No 6664 with an unidentified train at Tiddington station in 1959. Note the diminutive signal cabin and the goods yard on the right. (E.T. Gill/R.K. Blencowe Archive)

so that the driver and guard could set the brakes to regulate the speed and integrity of the train.

Tiddington was a small country station of wooden construction with an unusually short canopy. There was a single-road goods siding operated from the signal box that had been de-commissioned as a block post in the 1920s. Although only a modest station it served quite a large area, handling most of the milk traffic and transporting locally manufactured farming machinery.

The station was situated by the A418, Oxford Road, a short distance westward from the junction with Sandy Lane, where the site now is occupied by Sandy Lane Estate.

Leaving Tiddington there is a 3½-mile run through rolling countryside and over a double lattice girder bridge crossing the A40 to Wheatley, the next station on the line. Most of the middle section of line now lies beneath junctions 8 and 8A of the M40 motorway and the area occupied by Oxford Motorway Services. However, the railway bridge that spans Swaford Lane survives as a reminder of the railway that once passed this way.

After this the line continues on a rising gradient into Wheatley station, which was the first passing place after Thame. The station was located by a bridge carrying Ladder Hill Road over the railway and had Up and Down platforms with most of the infrastructure on the Up side, which, unusually, had no canopy. There was a two-road goods yard, also a goods shed, a cattle dock and a coal yard with land sale wharf.

Wheatley was famous for its stone quarrying, some of which was used to build Windsor Castle; however, the quarry men were also famous for their daily drinking binges, consuming gallons of ale at the ten pubs in the area!

Wheatley station closed to passengers on 7th January 1963 but the coal depot remained open until 19th May 1964, followed three years later by closure of the goods yard on 1st May 1967.

From Wheatley the line climbs gently to Shotover Hill and into a cutting that leads to Horspath Tunnel after which the line descends on a high embankment into Horspath Halt. The halt was almost identical to Towersey Halt and opened on the same day, 5th June 1933. This was in fact the second Horspath Halt to occupy this site. The first was built by the GWR in 1908, when steam railmotor services commenced, and halts were also

A general view of Wheatley station with an unidentified locomotive and train c1959. As the train gets the right away from the guard the fireman appears to check the coal bunker. (E.T. Gill/R.K. Blencowe Archive)

After Wheatley the next stop before Morris Cowley was another of the GWR-built halts, Horspath. This picture was taken in 1960 when passenger services were still operating, hence its good condition. The halt was in an elevated position above Cuddesdon Road. (Lens of Sutton Collection)

provided at Garsington Bridge and Iffley; all were closed on 22nd March 1913.

Horspath is an ancient English village set on the slopes of Shotover Hill. It has connections with some Oxford colleges, in particular Queen's College and the 15th-century 'Copcot Legend'. The legend tells of a student, John Copcot, who whilst reading his 'Aristotle' in Shotover Forest was attacked by a wild boar, at which point he shoved the book down its throat and 'the boar expired'. Every Christmas since, Queen's College has commemorated the legend by 'carrying in' a boar's head.

Today the area once occupied by Horspath Halt remains undeveloped and overgrown but the bridge under which Cuddesdon Road runs is still intact.

Leaving Horspath the next station was Morris Cowley, famous for its motor works. From the 1920s, together with its neighbour the Pressed Steel Company, it became the major employer in Oxford. William Morris started his business at the end of the 19th century, becoming well known in Oxford when he took up premises at 48 High Street. In 1913 the first Morris car was produced, with a total of 450 made that same year. Ten

One of the very few easily found remains of lost railways in Oxfordshire, the railway bridge spanning Cuddesdon Road at Horspath. In this view the halt was reached via a path to the right of the bridge, now obscured by trees. (Author)

years later the annual output had risen to 20,000 and in 1987 the production line turned out more than 450,000 vehicles.

Morris Cowley station opened on 24th September 1928 at the site of the former Garsington Bridge Halt. The station had a single platform, with a wooden building accommodating booking office, waiting rooms and toilet facilities. The factory had expanded significantly by this time and a signal box and additional sidings were added. The factory continued with its expansion to become a huge industrial complex with a web of sidings that were worked by the company's own locomotives.

Some of these engines were authorised by the GWR to operate over their metals and having first being inspected by GWR inspectors they were issued with a cast registration plate, not unlike a builder's plate. One such locomotive, 1943-built Peckett 0-4-0ST, works number 2047, was allocated plate number 276 authorising it to work 'Cowley Sidings'. This locomotive was subsequently exported to Australia, eventually finding its way into preservation at the Hunter Valley Steam Railway in New

Morris Cowley station in the 1950s and looking in pristine condition. Extensive sidings were provided here for the nearby motor works. Although Morris Cowley station has long since gone, the vast car complex is still in production, currently producing the modern 'Mini'. (Lens of Sutton Collection)

Peckett 0-4-0ST, one of the locomotives that worked the exchange sidings at Morris Cowley for a number of years, found its way halfway around the world to work in Australia. This picture shows the locomotive, now in preservation at the Hunter Valley Railway New South Wales. (Ed Slee)

The last station before Kennington Junction was Littlemore and in this view an unidentified train awaits departure for Oxford. (E.T. Gill/R.K. Blencowe Archive)

South Wales. It remains in New South Wales, having transferred to the Dorrig Steam Railway & Museum where it is in storage.

The next and last station on the line before Kennington Junction was Littlemore, 1½ miles from Morris Cowley. The brick-built station, which replaced the original wooden structure destroyed by fire, consisted of a booking office, waiting rooms and toilets, and unlike its predecessor had a canopy to its single platform. A modest single-road goods yard with a crane and weighbridge, together with a short private siding to the adjacent Littlemore Lunatic Asylum, completed its facilities. Littlemore station closed to passengers along with the others on the line on 7th January 1963 but remarkably the station building and part of the goods yard have survived and can be viewed from the original bridge that still carries Sandford Road over the railway.

From Littlemore the line descends briskly to cross the Thames via the unusually curved Kennington Viaduct to join the main line to Oxford.

3
Princes Risborough to Watlington

Princes Risborough station in the late 1920s, looking north from the end of the Up platform, with a GWR 'motor train' hauled by a '517' class 0-4-2T arriving from Aylesbury. Also in the view is the imposing North signal box behind which, on the extreme left, are the branches to Oxford and Watlington. (R.S. Carpenter Collection)

With the arrival of the Wycombe Railway in 1862, Princes Risborough went from a sleepy Buckinghamshire town to a significant railway junction with main lines to Birmingham and London, and branch lines to Aylesbury, Oxford and Watlington, all in the space of 45 years.

As for the branch to Watlington, this could have become a much grander scheme, as the Wallingford & Watlington Railway. This railway was authorised by Parliament in 1864 and would have created a through route from the Bristol–London main line, to the Wycombe Railway at Princes Risborough.

Much to the disappointment of Watlington folk this project was not progressed any further than the planning stage. However, they were determined to get their railway and the town's great and good enlisted the help of the former MP for Oxford (1837–1841) Thomas Augustus Parker, 6th Earl of Macclesfield, who lived at nearby Shirburn Castle. Together they promoted an independent railway company, the Watlington & Princes Risborough Railway (W&PRR), which eventually received Parliamentary approval on 26th July 1869.

Construction of this standard gauge single-track line took almost three years to complete. From Princes Risborough the alignment ran south-west, following the natural contours along the foot of the Chiltern Hills where no difficult terrain or significant engineering challenges were met. The line ran almost parallel with the Icknield Way, an ancient route once connecting Cromer in Norfolk with Avebury in Wiltshire. In the Middle Ages it was known as 'Acklin Street' and was not for the inexperienced traveller since it was a haven for highway robbery and the occasional murder!

Fortunately the railway builders were not troubled with these problems and the 9-mile branch line was opened on 15th August 1872, commencing public services with a 'one engine in steam' operation initially providing three trains per day, calling at intermediate stations at Chinnor and Aston Rowant. Although the residents of Watlington got their railway it terminated short of the town by ¾ mile, the station was in fact marginally closer to the villages of Pyrton and Shirburn.

Motive power was at first provided under an agreement with the GWR but in 1876 two Sharpe Stewart 2-4-0 side-tank locomotives were delivered new to the W&PRR as 'No 1' and 'No 2'.

Within ten years of starting the railway, however, the independent W&PRR experienced severe financial problems and finally, after some uncompromising negotiations, the GWR purchased the railway outright for £23,000, which was less than half the original expenditure required to build the line.

On 1st July 1883 the GWR became the new owners, beginning operations on 31st December that same year. Except for re-laying most of the original track there was no discernible improvement in either the service provision or passenger stock. In 1906 three halts were opened on the line and named 'Bledlow

Bridge Halt', 'Kingston Crossing Halt' and 'Lewknor Bridge Halt'. Nineteen years later the last passenger halt to be opened on the line was 'Wainhill Crossing'.

When originally built, the line was laid almost to Light Railway standard – a point that the GWR laboured during its negotiations with the W&PRR, claiming that they would need to utilise a particular type of locomotive with light axle loading to work the branch.

As it was, the GWR continued to use the W&PRR 2-4-0 tank engines, which they renumbered and operated on the line until 1899, at which time both locomotives were transferred to Swindon Works for a complete rebuild. One of these engines, No 1384, remained in service on the Watlington and two other branch lines until 1911 when the GWR sold it to the Bute Works Supply Co, from where it worked on the Weston, Clevedon & Portishead Railway (WC&PR) until its withdrawal in 1937.

Over the years a number of locomotive types were employed on the line but the main locomotive allocation was essentially a solitary 0-6-0 engine stabled at Watlington shed. Later, however, trains were in the charge of 57xx and 14xx tank engines hauling a single passenger coach. Some journeys were in fact operated with an auto-coach but on occasions, when suitably equipped locomotives were unavailable, the loco would run round its train at each terminus.

Prior to the grouping of all the independent railways into four big companies in 1923, the timetable consisted of five trains per day, weekdays only (Monday to Saturday), from Princes Risborough to Watlington and return, with the first train departing Watlington and Princes Risborough at 8.40 am and 10.02 am respectively. Although no Sunday service was provided, those residents of Watlington and Chinnor who commuted to London were adequately catered for. Apart from a well-timed morning connection at Princes Risborough, with the 'Breakfast Car Train' non-stop to Paddington, they could return on the 7.10 pm from Paddington, which had a 'slip carriage' provided. On arrival at Princes Risborough it would be 'slipped' (detached) for onward travel behind the 7.57 pm local train, arriving Watlington at 8.22 pm. A level of service that today would be unimaginable!

Goods trains usually ran, on average, twice per day carrying mainly farm produce, including milk trains, whilst lime and

A view of Watlington station's diminutive signal cabin (c1955) situated at the end of the platform. It is a GWR type 21 timber ground frame with a gabled roof that had holes drilled into it at the gable end for ventilation. (D.A.N. Ratcliffe/Kidderminster Railway Museum)

cement consignments were brought out of the cement works at Chinnor.

There was an interesting procedure on this line that involved the transport of a 'Travelling Railway Safe'. It required that on certain trains the guard would collect booking office cash from the various stations and take it down the line to Watlington where all the cash would be locked in the 'safe', which would then be placed on the train and transported back to Princes Risborough.

Ex-GWR 0-6-0PT No 4650 as it makes ready for a departure to Princes Risborough from Watlington on 21st May 1956. (Author's Collection)

Train services continued uninterrupted until 1st July 1957 when, in the face of diminishing passenger numbers, the line finally closed to passengers. The last train left Watlington, with its load of well-wishers and local dignitaries, ten minutes after its scheduled time of 9.00 am, arriving in Princes Risborough 25 minutes late. Thereafter, arrangements were made for rail replacement buses to take over and this was in the hands of City of Oxford Motor Services, service 88, consisting of five return journeys per day between Watlington and Princes Risborough. The bus service proved popular at the time since it provided low fares and convenient local pick up points, a luxury that Watlington residents did not enjoy with the railway.

Goods traffic over the line ended on 2nd January 1961 and the section of track between Watlington and Chinnor was lifted. However, the line from Chinnor to Princes Risborough lived on to serve the cement works until final closure in 1989. That same year the line was to take on a new role as a heritage line, when the Chinnor & Princes Risborough Railway Association was formed, and is now known as the 'Icknield Line'.

If we now take an imaginary journey down the line to Watlington, the train would start from the bay platform at

A view of Princes Risborough, looking north from the footbridge, as a Down freight waits at signals. Trains for Oxford or Watlington would depart from the platform at the extreme left of the picture and the branch lines can be seen bearing left behind the signal gantry. (F.W. Shuttleworth Collection)

Princes Risborough station that it also shared with the Thame–Oxford branch trains. Heading north past the substantial 100-lever North signal box, the line westwards stays on the left of the two tracks, which continue together for another ½ mile to Thame Junction, where the Thame–Oxford line continues ahead whilst the Watlington line turns south-west towards the first station, Bledlow Bridge Halt.

Bledlow had two stations, in fact, the first of which opened on the Oxford branch in 1862 but this lay over a mile from the village. Bledlow Bridge Halt on the other hand was closer, requiring only a few hundred yards walk from the centre of the village.

As the train headed towards Bledlow you could look out from your window, across open fields, to see a large cross carved into the chalk hill above Bledlow. Today the cross is still there and so are the remains of the halt, standing beside Penny Lane Bridge but no longer in use. From here the line crosses Water Lane Bridge, past Bledlow cricket ground, and then climbs steadily towards a short cutting to Wainhill Crossing.

A rare view of Bledlow Bridge Halt, which was the first stop on the Watlington branch. It was actually closer to the village of Bledlow than the 'other' Bledlow station situated on the Oxford branch. (Author's Collection)

Although Wainhill Crossing Halt has now been restored it is not open for passenger use and the crossing keeper's house is in private ownership.

The line descends now towards Chinnor, passing beneath the bridge carrying Station Road directly into the station, 3½ miles distant from Thame Junction. Chinnor station is now the headquarters of the Chinnor & Princes Risborough Railway (C&PRR).

The C&PRR took responsibility for the line between Chinnor and Thame Junction in 1990, only a few months after a BR train, consisting of 35 hoppers behind class 47 locomotive 47258, made a final trip to Chinnor cement works on 20th December 1989. Four years later, on 26th July 1994, the C&PRR acquired legal powers under a Transport & Works Order to operate passenger trains and on 20th August the first train operated the mile-long section between Chinnor to Wainhill Crossing Halt. By April 1995 this had been extended to two miles, terminating at Horsenden Lane and, by springtime 1996, the line had been extended to its current terminus at Thame Junction. Today the

A distant view of Chinnor station, c1967, with its single platform and the road leading to the cement works. (Brian Morgan/Kidderminster Railway Museum)

A marvellously rebuilt Chinnor station in 2009 and a vital part of the heritage line, the Chinnor & Princes Risborough Railway. (Author)

This is an early view, taken in 1919, of Kingston Crossing Halt, which was situated between Chinnor and Aston Rowant. (Locomotive & General Railway Photograph)

heritage railway is very popular and operates a variety of regular weekend steam and diesel services, together with special events. Chinnor station has also gained fame as a regular location for the TV series *Midsomer Murders*.

Leaving Chinnor, we continue for the next 1½ miles to Kingston Crossing Halt, situated at the junction of Swan's Way and Kingston Hill roads. This was a rail-level halt consisting of a low hard standing and a basic passenger shelter. Nothing remains of the halt or the crossing today that might indicate a railway once ran through this area.

Continuing south-west the line runs alongside the Ridgeway for one mile before entering the rather isolated Aston Rowant station, situated by the A40, London Road, and over a mile from the village.

A traditional brick-built structure, the station was full of character and during the post-war years it was used as a location for no fewer than four British feature films: *The Captive Heart* (1946), *My Brother Jonathan* (1947), *My Brother's Keeper* (1948) and *Portrait of Claire*, which was filmed in 1950. The site is now overgrown and nothing remains of the original station buildings

This is a view of Aston Rowant station taken on 3rd May 1959. It was built in 'Cottage Home' style with gabled roofs and large brick chimneystacks with ridge tiles and end finials. It has Gothic-style windows, one of which, at the nearside gable end, has been bricked-up at some time. Note the hand-cranked water pump. (D.A.N. Ratcliffe/Kidderminster Railway Museum)

A close-up view of Aston Rowant West signal cabin taken on 3rd May 1959. It is a GWR type 29 timber ground frame with gabled roof and is looking the worse for wear, having had all the windows and panels vandalised. (D.A.N. Ratcliffe/Kidderminster Railway Museum)

but the trackbed is still visible. It is a long-term goal of the C&PRR to extend its line to Aston Rowant and build a new station here.

As the line passes beneath the A40 road bridge, which is still in place but filled in to road level, the journey continues through open countryside for the next ¾ mile to the penultimate stop on the line, Lewknor Bridge Halt. This was another basic passenger halt, again built at rail-level; it was located near the junction of the B4009 and the unclassified Hill Road, and within walking distance of Lewknor village. Junction 6 of the M40 motorway now overshadows the site and this feature would be a major obstacle should the C&PRR wish to extend the railway further towards Watlington.

Leaving Lewknor Bridge Halt the line now runs parallel with the B4009 for the last 1¾ miles, passing Shirburn Castle on the way, before entering the terminus station at Watlington. This was the largest station on the branch, built in a secluded field ¾ mile from the town; today, 52 years after closure, most of the original structures remain hidden away in the undergrowth, including remnants of the station building and carriage shed, although they are all in various stages of dereliction.

A general view of Watlington station (c1967), looking back towards the stop blocks, with the coaling stage, carriage shed, station building and signal cabin. (Brian Morgan/Kidderminster Railway Museum)

Taken from the platform at Watlington c1967, this picture shows the corrugated iron clad carriage shed. (Brian Morgan/Kidderminster Railway Museum)

Watlington goods shed taken from the station approach road c.1967. A brick-built office/stores extension, with large chimney, was added at some time. (Brian Morgan/Kidderminster Railway Museum)

A view taken from the approach road of the main station buildings at Watlington and on the right is the rear part of the carriage shed, c1967. (Brian Morgan/Kidderminster Railway Museum)

This 'lost' railway has had an interesting life. Following the first eleven years of independent operation, the line was well patronised under the GWR, then after nationalisation the patronage declined until passenger services were eventually withdrawn; the line survived closure through a continued freight commitment from Chinnor and finally it returned to independent ownership and achieved heritage railway status – all in the space of 137 almost uninterrupted years!

Taken from approximately the same position, this is the view in 2009. Remarkably, hidden behind the trees and completely surrounded by vegetation, the carriage shed survives. (Author)

4
Cholsey, Moulsford & Wallingford Railway

A view from the platform at Cholsey & Moulsford station terminus of the Wallingford branch line. Standing in the bay platform is ex-GWR '1400' class 0-4-2T No 1444 waiting for a trip back to Wallingford. On the left is the London to Bristol main line. (John Marshall/Kidderminster Railway Museum)

Continuing the story from Chapter 3, the 2¾-mile Cholsey, Moulsford & Wallingford Railway started out in life in 1861 when it formed part of a scheme, promoted by an independent company made up of local business interests, to build a through route from the GWR Bristol–Paddington main line at Moulsford to the GWR's Wycombe line at Princes Risborough, routed via Wallingford, Benson, Watlington and Chinnor. It would also be the first standard gauge railway to interchange with the GWR's broad gauge system.

During the two years that followed, however, significant changes were made to the original scheme and a revised

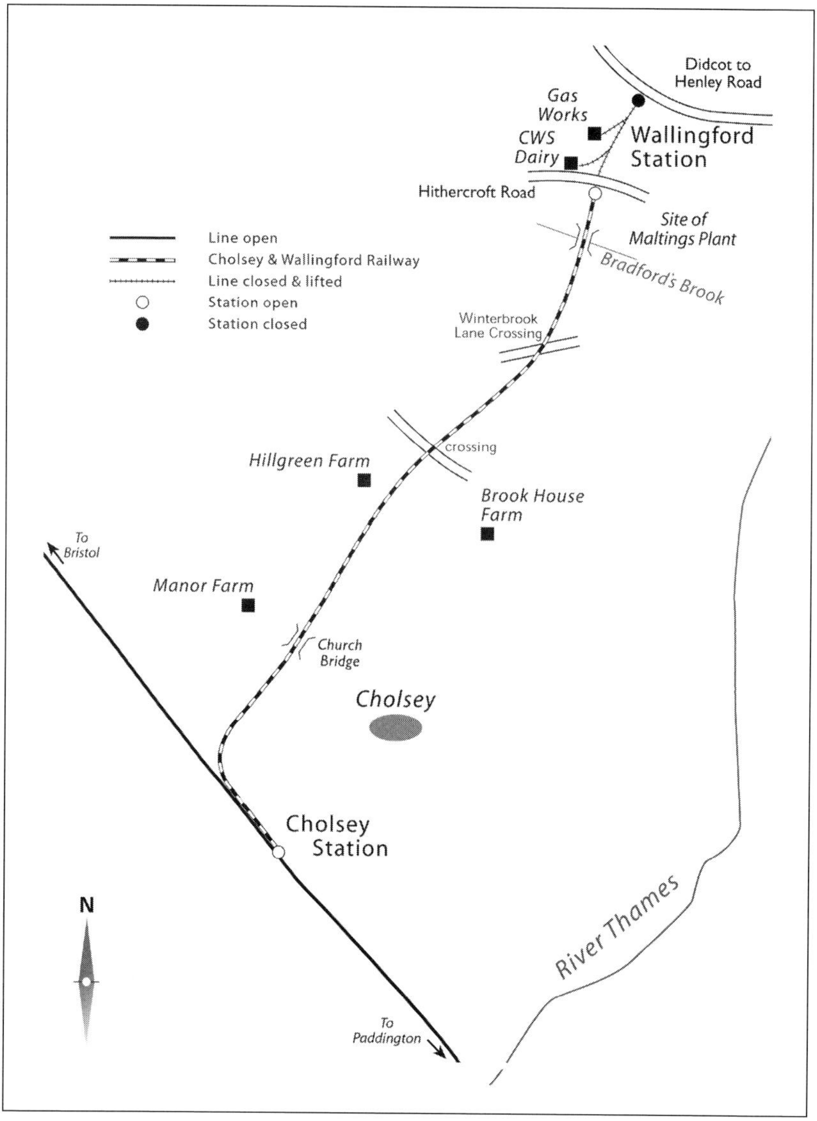

proposal, submitted in 1863, abridged the route to operate from a junction station on the London–Bristol main line named Wallingford Road, through to the town of Watlington. Construction work commenced in June 1864 and it was more than two years before the line opened, without any particular ceremony, on 7th July 1866 and then only as far as Wallingford, where a modest terminus station was built end-on to, and just short of, the Wallingford–Didcot road.

A working agreement had been arranged with the GWR to operate services over the line on behalf of the Wallingford Railway Company in return for a percentage of the passenger receipts.

In the first instance there were nine return journeys from the main line station to Wallingford each weekday (Monday to Saturday) and three on Sundays. Originally named Wallingford Road, the GWR changed this to 'Moulsford' on 2nd July 1866 to avoid timetable confusion with the new station.

Passenger numbers on the line, however, albeit steady, did not encourage the independent company to extend the line any further and in 1868 the directors agreed not to proceed beyond Wallingford. The company sold the line to the GWR on 25th July 1872, coincidentally the same year in which the independent Watlington & Princes Risborough Railway opened to passenger traffic.

The GWR operated the Wallingford branch relatively unchanged until 29th February 1892 when the original main line Moulsford station was closed and replaced by a brand new station, built at a point 55 chains west, and renamed 'Cholsey & Moulsford'.

For the next 67 years this was the main line terminus for the Wallingford branch and during that time, under the auspices of the GWR and BR Western Region, the line prospered, with respectable levels of passenger and goods traffic being maintained and at some point the railway even acquired an affectionate nickname, the 'Wallingford Bunk'.

In operational terms, the working timetable stated: 'SINGLE LINE worked by Train Staff, and only One Engine in Steam at a time, or two coupled together.' Details on motive power provision, particularly in the early years, are unclear but significant performers seemed to have been Armstrong's '517' class 0-4-2T and '850' class 0-6-0ST locomotives. Some of '517's were eventually converted to pannier tanks to overcome problems associated with the centre of gravity. However, from 1909 the line was worked almost exclusively by '517' class 0-4-2T tank locomotives until 1935 when '48xx' class 0-4-2T tank engines took over that role through to 1956, when Wallingford's single-road engine shed closed. Following this the supply of

Cholsey & Moulsford station in 1968, looking towards Didcot along the London–Bristol main line. The crowd of people on the right are standing by the bay platform for Wallingford, possibly waiting for an enthusiast's special working over the branch. (Rail Archive Stephenson)

An undated view of Wallingford's single-road engine shed with one of the line's auto-coaches standing in the siding. The station building is to the right of the coach.

An interesting view of Wallingford Station Box taken on 22nd July 1958, with the goods shed in the background and what appears to be a substantial yard crane. (Rail Archive Stephenson)

locomotives for the branch changed from Reading to Didcot, from which came a number of different types to work the line, including Collett 0-6-0 tender engines.

In the mid 1950s competing bus services took their toll on the railways and post-war prosperity led to a rise in the availability of private motorcars, which together brought about a decline in passenger revenue on the branch line that resulted in passenger services being withdrawn. The last passenger train ran from Wallingford on 15th June 1959 and goods trains ceased operations to Wallingford station on 13th September 1965.

However, a fortunate turn of events took place during 1961 when a new Associated British Maltsters plant was built alongside the line just south of Wallingford station and part of that development included a requirement for a connection to the existing railway. Unfortunately, this did not save the old station and it was demolished in 1969 but the railway continued to serve the factory and secured the line's survival until 1981 when the maltings plant changed its transport logistics by transferring its products from rail to road transport.

As a consequence the line closed and BR even ran a final

enthusiasts' special, 'The Wallingford Wake', on 31st May 1981. Standing in the wings, however, was a group of railway enthusiasts who by then had formed the Cholsey & Wallingford Railway Preservation Society (C&WRPS) and they had their sights firmly set on acquiring the line for preservation.

During the next four years the group concentrated on preparing the line at the Wallingford site for visitors and in 1985 modest train rides were run for the public, hauled by a class 08 shunter. After a further 12 years' hard work the line was opened throughout and passenger services were restored all the way to Cholsey, even terminating in the original bay platform.

Wallingford station in the early 1950s would have been a hive of activity. The station environs accommodated a number of sidings serving a substantial goods shed and a land sale wharf used by local coal merchants, two of which operated their own private-owner coal wagons. The station had one 309-ft-long platform opposite a single-road engine shed (GWR No 161), which was adjacent to a siding that served Wallingford's Gas & Coke Company.

Starting our imaginary journey from Wallingford the train, having passed the station's 13-lever signal box, heads south-west. After approximately ¼ mile the Cooperative Wholesale Society's creamery and private siding is reached before the line passes beneath the bridge carrying Hithercroft Road. When this road was upgraded in the late 1960s the bridge was removed, severing the railway at this point and making the Associated British Maltsters plant a new terminus for the branch line and now the site of the C&WRPS Wallingford station and operating centre.

Immediately after the bridge our train crosses Bradford's Brook, a tributary of the River Thames, and from this point the line runs at a shallow descending gradient into open countryside before negotiating an occupation crossing over Winterbrook Lane. Some years ago the Wallingford bypass was built near here, which could have had disastrous consequences for the heritage railway had it not been for C&WRPS members successfully reaching an agreement with the highway planners for a modern barrier crossing to be installed.

From Winterbrook Lane our train continues south-west, over Green Lane Crossing, and ambles through pleasant undulating farmland for ½ mile before negotiating Church Bridge, which is the only over-bridge on the line. Once across the bridge the

On 21st June 1969 a three-car DMU ventures onto the Cholsey & Wallingford branch line with an unidentified enthusiast's special and is seen here ambling towards Cholsey. (Steve Davies Collection)

railway climbs at 1:200, turning south, before levelling out and running alongside the Bristol–Paddington main line for a short distance. It then rolls into the Up bay platform at Cholsey station, which has remained largely unchanged from when it was originally built. From here passengers can connect with trains currently operated by First Great Western. For Agatha Christie fans there is Cholsey parish church where the author's grave can be found in the well-kept churchyard.

So, this 'lost' railway has a new life now and like so many of the heritage lines it has survived a number of events, not least the timely intervention of a group of dedicated railway enthusiasts who have secured its future.

5
The Wantage Tramway

A picture taken for the Wantage Tramway Company in 1900 at Oxford Lane with Mathews 'Box' engine No 6 and 2nd car No 5 (1912–1925). (Wantage Museum)

As passengers board the Eurostar train at St Pancras station for a 21st-century railway journey to the near continent, little thought will be given to the bronze statue of John Betjeman, Poet Laureate (1972–1984) and one of the country's greatest railway devotees who, for a long time, resided in Wantage, where he is now honoured by a memorial park named after him.

When Brunel's London to Bristol main line opened the section west of Steventon in 1840 it bypassed Wantage by just 2½ miles and the coming of the railway age left the town's residents feeling a little isolated. However, on 10th November 1873 the Wantage Tramway Company Ltd had been incorporated and with a working capital of £9,970 it planned to build a 2½-mile standard gauge line from the GWR's main line at Wantage Road station to Wantage town where a terminus station was to be constructed in Mill Street.

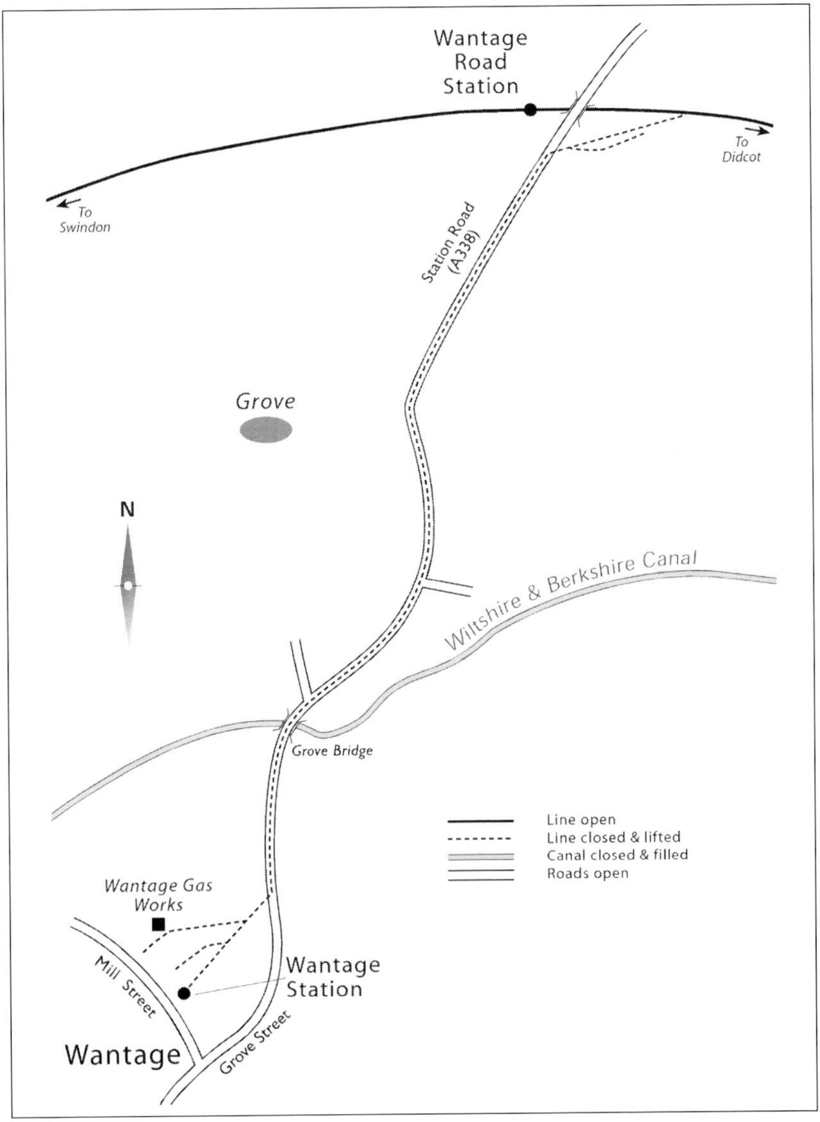

The proposal for a tramway was submitted to the Board of Trade, with a provisional order passed in March 1874 and on 7th August 1874 the railway received Royal Assent. Construction started in December 1874 and following eight months of intense building work the Wantage Tramway was completed and opened to traffic on 1st October 1875, initially as a horse tramway to convey goods only.

During the following year, however, the tramway company sought Parliamentary approval for the use of mechanical traction and Royal Assent was given on 27th June 1876. In anticipation of this approval, the company had already undertaken trials (over track laid on land wholly owned by the tramway) with a steam tramcar that was built to a design of an early shipbuilding engineer, John Grantham. The tramcar was built by the Oldbury Carriage Works and measured approximately 30 ft long, with seats for 44 people, 24 of which were on the exterior. The steam engine and twin upright boilers, built by Merryweather of Greenwich, were positioned in a separate compartment midway along the car. At that time, given the smoke and soot that would be generated by such a machine, it must have been an interesting ride, particularly for those outside!

Unfortunately, the tramcar functioned reliably for only a short time and the steep gradient on the line brought about its eventual failure. Not to be defeated, however, the company had the car rebuilt with new wheels, its body shortened to 27 ft 3 ins and fitted with a new large single vertical boiler made by London fire engine builders Shand & Mason.

This rebuilt tramcar came into regular service on 1st August 1876 and would remain in passenger service on the Wantage Tramway for the next two years. Thereafter a number of different trams and tram engines were acquired for use on the railway. The first 'standard' locomotive purchased for the line was No 5, a diminutive 0-4-0 well tank, built in 1857 by George England & Co of Hatcham Ironworks, New Cross, London. Before its arrival in Wantage this locomotive had acquired an interesting history. It was built initially to work the 4-mile long Sandy and Potton Railway in Bedfordshire where it also carried the name *Shannon*. On 7th July 1862 that branch line became part of the London & North Western Railway (LNWR) Cambridge to Bedford line where in fact the LNWR removed the locomotive's nameplate and replaced it with just a running number, No 1104.

In less than a year the locomotive made a very brief and operationally unsuccessful period on the Cromford & High Peak Railway before being transferred to Crewe where it worked as station pilot until 1878. During that same year, whilst at Crewe,

On 8th January 1936, Wantage Tramway's locomotive No 5 came to grief near Elms Road and brought its train of coal wagons off the track by the site of the new Elms Farm Model Dairy. (F.E.J. Burgiss)

the Wantage Tramway acquired No 1104 for the princely sum of £350 and it became Wantage No 5 and known with affection by local residents as *Jane*. This locomotive worked on the line continuously until 1945, interrupted only for a number of rebuilds at Swindon works, when it was finally withdrawn from traffic and stored at Wantage.

As steam traction took over from horse-drawn traction the additional weight of steam trams and locomotives, hauling what were essentially converted streetcars, created problems concerning the weight of these vehicles travelling along the route. This was particularly evident near Grove where the bridge carrying the road and railway over the Wiltshire & Berkshire Canal branch seemed to be at risk and needed replacing. The new bridge, which was manufactured and installed by Alfred Anderton & Sons based in Accrington, was later passed for use by Board of Trade Inspector, Major General C.S. Hutchinson RE.

In 1847, as Wantage began to illuminate its streets by gas lamps, the newly established Wantage Gas Works received its coal via a branch of the Wiltshire & Berkshire Canal and this remained the

On 30th July 1938 Manning Wardle 0-4-0ST No 7 is photographed at Grove Bridge approaching Wantage goods yard. A man on a bicycle (possibly a railway worker) and what appears to be an army truck stop to allow the train to pass. (L.W. Perkins/Kidderminster Railway Museum)

mode of transport for the next 30 years. When the Wantage Tramway commenced operations, it quickly secured its position as a cost-effective alternative to canal transport. At this point the gas works embarked on an arrangement with the tramway company to convey by rail all its coal requirements to the works and remove the various by-products off site, also by rail.

In 1880 the tramway had a momentary flirtation with Mekaski compressed air engines, which proved to be a spectacular failure. Not only did they run out of air before completing a trip but the air compressor used more coal than the fleet of steam engines!

At the turn of the century, passenger operations on the tramway were consistently well patronised with eleven return trips per day, Monday to Saturday, between Wantage and Wantage Road station. Although there was no Sunday service the tramway frequently adjusted the weekday timetable in order to coincide with main line arrivals and departures at Wantage Road station.

The Great War (1914–18) took its toll on the tramway, bringing about significant losses in revenue and in the early 1920s the development of omnibus routes into the Wantage/Grove area. The buses, ironically promoted and operated by the GWR, offered frequent services and a range of destinations that

Near to Wantage Road station, Wantage Tramway Company's Hughes tram engine No 3 with tramcars No 1 and No 4 pause for the camera c1905. (F.E.J. Burgiss)

Manning Wardle 0-4-0ST No 7 in 1920, seen here after arriving at the GWR Wantage Road station yard with cars No 5 and No 4 attached. The driver, guard and porter with sack truck pose for the camera and in the background is the Wantage Road signal box, a goods shed and a yard crane. (Wantage Museum)

A wonderful picture of Wantage Tramway's Town terminal taken in 1925, during the last year of passenger operations, with tramcar No 3, engine No 6 and car No 5. (Wantage Museum)

On the same day as the above picture Mr Hewitt and driver Mr Weaving pose for a close up, with Mathews 'Box' engine No 6 – and revealing that even in those days advertising was as important as it is today. (Wantage Museum)

would eventually abstract further revenue from the tramway, to such an extent that passenger services on the line were withdrawn entirely on 1st August 1925.

On the freight side, the tramway had created an almost symbiotic relationship with its customers, particularly Wantage Gas Works, Clark's flour mill and a number of local coal and timber merchants, and by 1910 the tramway was handling more than 5,000 wagonloads of freight. Unfortunately in 1945, as the tramway recovered from wartime austerity, including a four-month closure (November 1943 to February 1944) as work took place at Grove Airfield, Wantage Gas Works was contemplating a buy-out proposed by the Oxford Gas Company.

After this, the tramway never really recovered its pre-war prosperity and with the permanent way in a poor state of repair and both locomotives, No 5 and No 7, suffering from a lack of regular maintenance the directors decided to close down the operation. As a consequence the Wantage Tramway, an independent and profitable railway company throughout its 70-year life, closed completely on 19th December 1945.

Following closure, the two steam locomotives were disposed

Wantage Tramway Manning Wardle 0-4-0ST No 7, built in 1888, shunting wagons at Wantage on 30th July 1938. Attached to the engine is a private owner wagon belonging to Hall & Sons, a long way from its hometown of Macclesfield. (V.R. Webster/Kidderminster Railway Museum)

Manning Wardle 0-4-0ST No 7 and tramcar No 4 pose for the photographer as it makes a stop at Grove, near Oxford Road, with the driver, guard and a passenger of Chapman & Sons, c1925. (Wantage Museum)

of with little ceremony on 25th April 1946. Manning Wardle 0-4-0 No 7 was sold to A.R. Adams & Son of Newport but was scrapped a few years later. Fortunately, the fate of No 5 was to become entirely different as it was purchased by the GWR for £100 and placed on display at their Wantage Road station, acquiring its original name – *Shannon*.

She remained there until 1965 when the Beeching axe descended and closed the station. Luckily, a number of railway enthusiasts were on hand to recognise the locomotive's significant historic importance and in the short term a need for it to be moved to a secure place. The United Kingdom Atomic Energy Authority came to the rescue and offered to store the locomotive at their facility based in Grove; she stayed there until 18 January 1969 when she was transported by road to her new home at the Great Western Society's Didcot shed.

A few years later, at the age of 118, *Shannon*, having earned a place in railway history, took part in the 150th anniversary of the Stockton & Darlington Railway celebrations where she was in steam once again to join the cavalcade of locomotives that paraded at Shildon, before enormous crowds of enthusiasts, on 31st August 1975.

A picture of Wantage Road signal box taken c1965, about the time that MAS (Manufacturing Advisory Service) signalling was being introduced, and shows the web of lines controlled from this box. In the background the road to Wantage runs from right to left. (F.W. Shuttleworth Collection)

A great piece of GWR architecture in the shape of the goods transhipment shed at Wantage Road station c1965. (F.W. Shuttleworth Collection)

This is a substantial hand-cranked yard crane at Wantage Road station sidings and coal wharf, still in use in 1965 when this picture was taken. (F.W. Shuttleworth Collection)

Today *Shannon* lives on, as part of the National Collection at the Didcot Railway Centre, but little remains of the Wantage Tramway other than the 1904-built Wantage Tramway Office building in Mill Street. Even this has been structurally altered over the years but it still bears a carved stone panel showing the company's name and date. To the passing railway enthusiast, there is no other indication that a small but busy railway once connected the town with Brunel's main line to London.

6
Uffington to Faringdon

A view of Faringdon station on 26th April 1959 as a two-coach train works a Railway Enthusiasts' Club special over the branch line behind ex-GWR '1361' class 0-6-0ST, No 1365. The station building is seen in the background. (John Marshall/Kidderminster Railway Museum)

Tuesday was a special day on the Faringdon branch line for it was the day on which, ever since the Reformation, various historic public gatherings had been held in Faringdon. These included Candelmas Day, 18th February, the Tuesday following Whitsun, 13th October (St Luke's Day) and other Tuesdays involving the weekly fairs and the employment assemblies held in the town. Accordingly, as the branch line opened to passenger services it was to have special regard for Tuesday by providing in the timetable an additional journey on the first Tuesday of each month, an arrangement that lasted until 19th September 1934 when the eleven return journeys per day, Monday to Saturday, were reduced to just four trips.

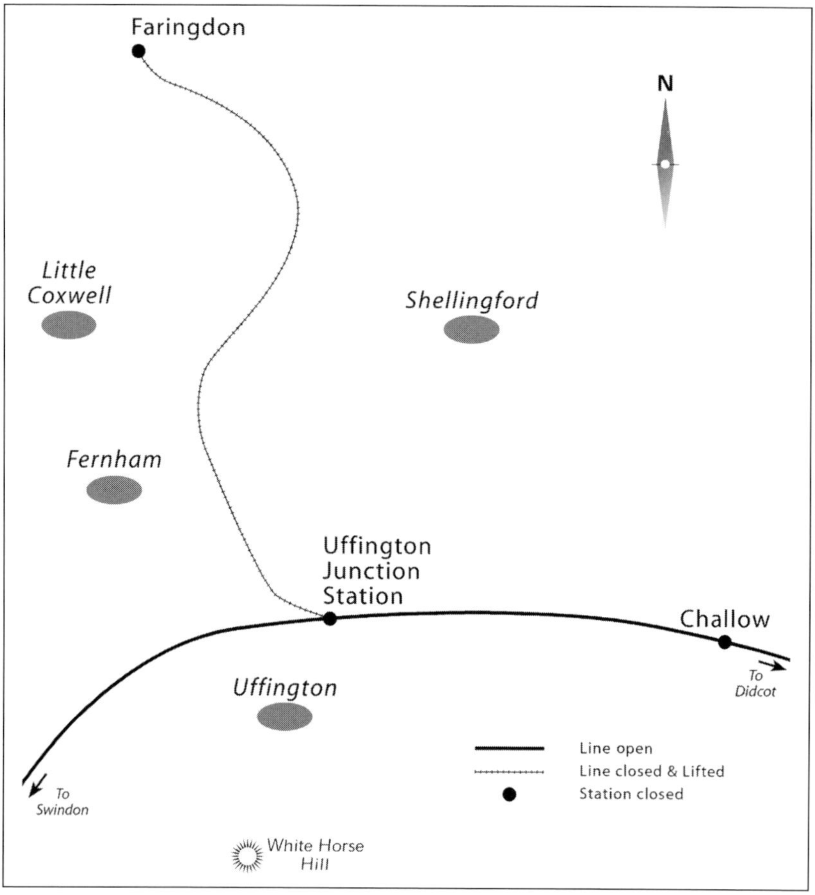

The 3½-mile branch line was, in fact, the result of a private company formed by a group of local individuals and businessmen to open up valuable farming areas. The proposals to build the line were submitted during 1859 at a time when 'railway mania' had gripped the country and dozens of similar schemes were being placed before Parliament.

The Faringdon branch proposal succeeded, however, and Royal Assent was given to the Faringdon Railway Company in August 1860 to build a broad gauge line from Faringdon, at a place called 'The Butts', to a junction with the GWR's main Paddington– Bristol line situated at Moor Mill one mile north of the village of Uffington.

Before construction could commence, tenders were invited from contractors who had expressed an interest in building the line and the lowest of four tenders received was from a Mr Lewis of Carmarthen. The board of directors, chaired by Mr David Bennett, accepted this tender on 12th November 1860.

From hereon, David Bennett led the company from one minor crisis to another as he attempted to raise the necessary funds, sometimes enticing reluctant shareholders with less than honest statements and dubious promises. At this time the purchase price of some of the land necessary to build the railway was also taking its toll on available cash and after the first six months the contractor had not laid a foot of track.

By April 1861 the Faringdon Company was desperately trying to enlist the help of the GWR to build the junction station, on the grounds that it would benefit both companies and remarkably the GWR agreed; the proposed station was named after the nearest village, Uffington.

The village of Uffington nestles in the shadow of the White Horse Hills in an area once known as Ock Valley. It is home to one of England's most famous and ancient sites, the 374-ft-long figure of a white horse, which was cut into the chalk hillside above the village of Woolstone during the Bronze Age.

Uffington station, the GWR decided, was not going to replace the already established Faringdon Road main line station, situated 3 miles east; instead the GWR decided Faringdon Road station should remain open but be renamed 'Challow'.

Construction of the branch continued, with some tangible evidence of the works appearing during the summer of 1861. But it was a slow affair, mostly due to the contractor, Mr Lewis, not having sufficient materials available through constantly being kept short of money by the Faringdon Company directors.

In September 1861, as the branch line was beginning to take shape, the Faringdon Company was contacted by the East Gloucestershire Railway (EGR) to advise the Faringdon directors that the EGR was planning to build a new line from Cheltenham to Faringdon. This would, in fact, provide an opportunity for a through route from Wales to London with the Faringdon branch making the final link with the GWR main line at Uffington Junction.

The Faringdon directors were not entirely happy with such an amalgamation and submitted their own financial proposal to the

The original Faringdon Road station was renamed Challow on 1st June 1864 to avoid any confusion with Faringdon station on the branch from Uffington. This is a view of the derelict Challow station in the mid 1960s. (Author's Collection)

EGR, which was met with great disapproval. Not to be held back, the EGR then approached the GWR with a similar scheme but one that isolated the Faringdon Railway. Although the GWR recognised some merit in this proposal it laid down certain conditions that were unacceptable to the EGR, and although the scheme endured for another two years and almost gained Parliamentary approval, it was pursued no further.

As April 1862 approached, the contractor stopped work on the line since he had again been denied funds from the Faringdon Company. It was almost a year before Lewis returned to resume work on the railway, following a written assurance that the money owed to him would be paid.

Work started again on 3rd March 1863 and by the end of April the majority of the groundwork between Moor Mill and Faringdon was complete. Construction continued throughout 1863 and by the end of March 1864 the line had been finished and the passenger stations were ready for occupation. In view of this the Faringdon Company invited the Board of Trade to inspect their railway for public passenger use.

On 13th April 1864 the Board of Trade dispatched their Inspector, Captain F.H. Rich RE, to Faringdon. However,

Captain Rich was unimpressed with what he had scrutinised and decided that the railway did not meet the standards required for public use. His report, in fact, referred to no fewer than ten areas of concern to be put right by the Faringdon Company. Captain Rich returned to Faringdon the following month to follow up his recommendations and duly passed the line as fit for public service.

A few weeks later, on 1st June 1864, the Faringdon Railway ran its first passenger service, with the customary military band and host of invited guests, and the day was even declared a public holiday.

Back in Paddington the directors and shareholders of the GWR, chaired by Daniel Gooch, were discussing the request from the Faringdon Company for the GWR to provide the necessary locomotives and stock to operate the branch line on their behalf. It was proposed that the GWR would take 55% of the revenue received and, over the first year of operation, would require a guaranteed minimum sum of £1,040 should the receipts fall short of the 55%. Gooch supported the arrangement and following a vote it was carried almost unanimously.

And so, the people of Faringdon got their own railway with a timetable consisting of four return workings on weekdays (Monday to Saturday) and three trips (commencing midday) on Sundays. The following month that was increased to seven return trips weekdays, with Sundays remaining the same.

As it turned out the revenue taken on the railway never reached the GWR's requisite £1,040 per mile but in 1870 the takings reached a one-time high of £2,300, from which the GWR duly took its 55% share.

The Faringdon shareholders, on the other hand, never received a penny of the dividends that were pledged by the Faringdon chairman at the time the shareholders handed over their investments. Also the directors were lacklustre throughout in the company's management and seemingly reckless in not paying their creditors.

By 1872 the GWR was already in the process of converting the main line to mixed gauge and as this progressed the number of standard gauge trains began to increase, displacing the broad gauge workings. At Faringdon the question of gauge conversion was discussed but by and large there was no immediate plan to carry out the work. The conversion was delayed, even in the face of increased time and inconvenience to customers as goods were transhipped at Uffington from broad gauge wagons (off the branch) to the new standard gauge stock for the main line.

Eventually (after 6 years!) the decision was made to re-gauge the branch line and this took place during 26th and 27th July 1878 and, for that brief time, stagecoaches were hired to operate 'rail replacement' services during the closure. At the same time the company decided to build an interlocking 10-lever signal box at Faringdon, together with modern telegraph instruments to communicate with Uffington signal box.

Three years earlier, in 1875, the GWR made an offer to the Faringdon shareholders to take over the branch line outright, offering GWR shares in exchange for their holdings in the Faringdon Railway Company. Although the Faringdon shareholders were indeed happy with this arrangement, with an expectation that they would at last receive dividend payments in the future, the Faringdon directors were not and attempted to pass on to the GWR their accrued liabilities and debts as part of the deal. The GWR was having none of it and the proposal fell through.

Another eleven years were to pass before, in sheer frustration, the Faringdon shareholders, following a unanimous vote, demanded that the directors submit to the GWR an agreement, which the shareholders had themselves prepared, authorising the take-over of the Faringdon Railway. This document was sent, under the company seal, to the GWR at Paddington on 17th June 1886 and the following month the GWR became the new owner of the Uffington–Faringdon branch line.

Ten years on, the Faringdon branch timetable consisted of thirteen return trips on Monday to Saturday, with two on Sundays and additional trips morning and afternoon on the first Tuesday of each month.

The coming of the railway to Faringdon brought additional economic activity to the town and the speed at which goods could be moved around, particularly perishables, meant that a high street fishmonger (hitherto confined to towns and villages near the sea) could prosper, although in an inland town. Other businesses in the area benefited from the railway's haulage capability, and customers included a local iron foundry, an agricultural machinery works and a sawmill.

From this point on, the Faringdon branch line entered four

Whilst still open to all services, c1957–1960, a view of the station frontage at Faringdon, photographed from Station Road. (R.S. Carpenter)

A general view of Faringdon station, looking towards the stop blocks and the forecourt off Station Road. 31st March 1962. (G.E.S. Parker//Kidderminster Railway Museum)

decades of relative stability and although never achieving record numbers of passengers (averaging 60 per weekday) the freight side of the business exceeded 380 tons departing Faringdon each weekday.

Faringdon station had all the attributes of a busy country terminus, with a main platform approximately 300-ft long and a short bay of around 60 ft. The station building, which still stands and is currently occupied by a local nursery school, is an interesting structure. A Witney-based stonemason, Malachi Bartlett, using limestone that was quarried in Witney, built the station to an unusual design that utilised a double-pitched roof where each side met at the middle of the structure and projected outward to form a canopy at the platform and entrance elevations.

Other facilities included a single-road engine shed, built for a broad gauge locomotive, a goods shed, a coaling stage, a cattle dock and a siding to the local sawmill/timber merchants.

At the turn of the century, the line was being worked mostly by a number of Armstrong's class '517' 0-4-2 side tank locomotives and 'Metro' 2-4-0 side tanks, although it is unlikely that the 'Metros' were residents of the Faringdon shed. From the

Whilst the branch line was still open to all services this view of Faringdon station shows the loco shed, bay platform and goods shed c1957–1960. (R.S. Carpenter)

A 1950s' view of the London to Bristol main line at Uffington as 'Hall' class 4-6-0 No 6924 'Grantley Hall' storms past the station on its way back to Swindon following a running in turn. (Author's Collection)

1920s a number of 0-6-0PT pannier locomotives worked the branch, usually with one coach or a mixed arrangement of coach and wagons depending on requirements.

The branch was particularly busy throughout the Second World War with extra milk traffic but as the war ended there was a general decline in passenger usage, mostly brought on by a local bus service, which covered the villages between Faringdon, Uffington and Challow. Although the goods traffic was holding up and providing respectable revenue, the post-war availability of private motorcars added to the decline of passenger services. Even the intervention by British Railways, with its robust promotion of the railway, did not help and, on 11th November 1951, a meeting was called at Swindon to discuss the future of the Faringdon branch. British Railways officials set out the impoverished situation with regard to passenger receipts, against the costs of running the service. Whilst members of the Faringdon Town Council were present at that meeting, no objections were made to the line's closure; their only concern was that the bus service should be improved!

Uffington signal box, c1965, situated on the Up side of the London–Bristol main line, with the remains of the Faringdon branch running behind the box; all track had been lifted. (Author's Collection)

Faringdon station on 31st March 1962, three months after closure to passengers, but goods vans in the siding indicate that the station was still in use for freight traffic. (G.E.S Parker/Kidderminster Railway Museum)

A view from the platform at Uffington station on 13th May 1961 with a Railway Club Special awaiting departure for a 'Brake Van' trip over the branch to Faringdon. The locomotive is '1600' class 0-6-0PT No 1658 and interestingly the rear brake van W68748 bears the legend 'Oxley Sidings Not in Common Use'. (D.A.N. Ratcliffe/Kidderminster Railway Museum)

Nothing more being said, the last passenger train operated over the line on Saturday, 29th December 1951, ironically to a large crowd of people congregated at Faringdon to see the train away. The line continued as a goods-only line for another 12 years when finally the Beeching axe descended on the branch, bringing its closure on 1st July 1963.

Today little evidence of the branch line exists other than the station building at Faringdon. The station yard accommodates a commercial development but there are no immediately identifiable remains of the trackbed or its alignment towards Uffington, where the station is but a memory. The site is now part of Uffington Trading Estate but a section of the road leading down to the original crossing over the main line can still be seen, and the road bridge that replaced it is still in use.

Apart from that, this really is a lost railway.

Ex-GWR '1600' class 0-6-0PT No 1658 at Faringdon with a Gloucester Railway Society special on 31st March 1962. (R.J. Leonard/Kidderminster Railway Museum)

Uffington station with the Gloucester Railway Society special on 31st March 1962. (R.J. Leonard/ Kidderminster Railway Museum)

7
Radley to Abingdon

Abingdon station in April 1961 as '1400' class 0-4-2T No 1450 propels its branch train to Radley.

Railway schemes in the 1830s did not always find favour or enthusiasm from every town or village in the land. However, as the railways developed, the benefits that they brought summoned a change of mind for some of these towns.

One of these was Abingdon, county town of Berkshire since receiving its Royal Charter in 1556, which had earlier opposed the GWR's planned railway between the Bristol main line and Oxford running through or near Abingdon, petitioning Parliament against two separate proposals, submitted in 1837 and 1838 respectively.

Four years later Abingdon Town Council sought a meeting with the GWR to consider the possibility of aligning the projected Didcot–Oxford line nearer to Abingdon for the benefit of the townsfolk. The GWR were very positive about this and in the following year they were prepared to include a branch line into Abingdon as part of the Didcot–Oxford railway.

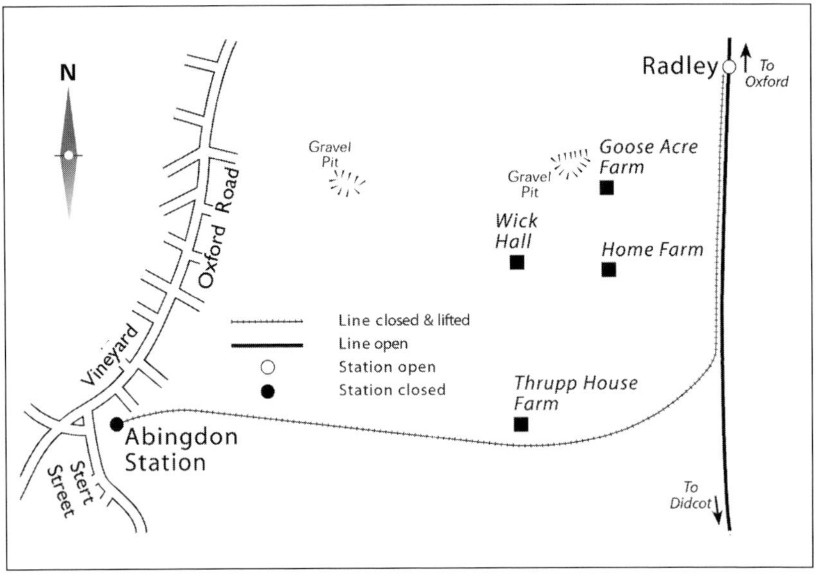

Astonishingly, the Town Council had a change of mind and voted against the scheme. After this bizarre rebuttal the GWR did not consider any further proposals that included Abingdon. Like the proverbial elephant the GWR never forgot this and in the *Official Guide to the Great Western Railway 1860*, the town was referred to as 'Quiet, clean and dull in Abingdon now ... There is little to detain the stranger in Abingdon ...'. It is widely held that Abingdon's failure to embrace the railway revolution brought about the town's loss of status when, in 1867 Reading became the new county town for Berkshire.

Early in 1855, however, Abingdon's great and good decided that the township could quickly become isolated and they had a change of heart; a scheme was subsequently approved to form the Abingdon Railway Company. This was eventually authorised on 15th June 1855 and the 1¾-mile branch line, from a junction with the Didcot–Oxford main line at Nuneham to a terminus station in the centre of Abingdon, was completed in less than 12 months.

For the purchase price of £472, the Town Council provided the Abingdon Railway with a plot of land, just off Stert Street, to accommodate the station and a substantial goods yard. The line finally opened on 2nd June 1856 and became the earliest branch line in the area. The railway was laid to broad gauge and the Abingdon Railway Company reached an agreement with the GWR to provide the motive power and stock to operate the passenger and goods service.

On that opening day the GWR ran the first train with a Gooch-designed 2-2-2 locomotive, *Eagle*, which was built in 1838 by Sharp, Roberts and Company. The early passenger service was a modest affair with eight weekday return trips and two on Sundays.

In 1865 Abingdon Town Council, now extremely enthusiastic about their railway, discovered that Oxford City Council and the University authorities were both undivided in their opposition to a carriage & wagon works, planned by the GWR, being sited near the city. Grasping the moment, Abingdon Town Council advised the GWR that they had land and cash to offer should the GWR wish to relocate the planned works to an area approximately ¼ mile east of Abingdon station. Although the GWR considered this, particularly in view of the concessions available, they decided that there was an unacceptable risk of flooding in this particular area and declined Abingdon's generous offer.

On 26th November 1872 the line was re-gauged to 4 ft 8½ ins and the following year the junction at Nuneham was disconnected and its station, composed only of basic wooden platforms, was closed. The branch line was then extended ¾ mile northwards, running alongside the Oxford–Didcot main line to a newly-built station at Radley. Here, a bay platform was provided for Abingdon trains and on its opening on 8th September 1873 a revised timetable increased the passenger service to ten return trips per weekday (Monday to Saturday) and four on Sundays.

The service from Radley continued generally unaltered until 1876 when the timetable was enhanced further to fifteen return trains each weekday and five on Sunday.

In 1929 the famous MG cars factory opened in Abingdon, with the works situated between Cemetery Road and Marcham Road. MG survived until 1979 and during those 50 years the company had been a good customer for the railway, shipping most of its cars out of Abingdon by rail.

Abingdon station, with its single platform, was both neat and functional and originally constructed of wood and brick, with an

An interesting street side view of the new buildings at Abingdon station c1909, which was just after it was rebuilt following a runaway accident that partially demolished the original timber structure. (Kidderminster Railway Museum)

Abingdon station (c1949–1951) looking towards Radley, showing the station yard, signal box and the original engine shed. (Joe Moss Collection)

overall timber roof. In 1908, however, a shunting accident, involving wagons that were propelled into carriages standing at the platform, caused major structural damage to the station.

Only four years earlier the Abingdon Railway Company had sold their interests to the GWR and it fell upon this company to rebuild the station. The work was completed in the summer of 1908 and for a country branch line it was to a high standard, built entirely of brick with a slate roof and the platform furnished with a single canopy.

The sizeable station yard consisted of a goods shed, a single-road engine shed that was built to broad gauge (leaving room to spare for servicing standard gauge locomotives) and sidings to the local gas works and malthouse, together with a substantial coal yard, all controlled by a small signal cabin.

The branch line itself had no significant engineering features and, with a ruling gradient of 1 in 200, it was no severe challenge for enginemen. After the line was re-gauged in 1872 the branch was worked by Armstrong's '517' class 0-4-2-T locomotives and they remained as the principal motive power until 1947. As nationalisation came in 1948 the allocation changed to '1400' class 0-4-2T engines and the '5800' class 0-4-2T locomotives.

A picture of Abingdon station approach, taken c1965, showing the yard area and goods shed with the signal box and station visible in the background. (F.W. Shuttleworth Collection)

A general view of Abingdon station, thought to be c1960, showing the side and rear canopies and bay platforms.

Looking south at Radley station on 12th May 1963 with the Oxford–Didcot main line on the left running through the station and the Abingdon platform and line on the right. An attractive GWR bracket signal dominates the view and the station running-in board bears the legend 'Radley Junction for Abingdon'. (P.J. Garland Collection)

Abingdon station on 5th September 1963 with '5700' class 0-6-0PT No 4649 running around freight from Oxford. Note the Austin cars and Ford van on the platform area, together with the railway's 'competition'. (P.J. Garland Collection)

A detailed view of the goods shed at Abingdon station (c1965). The shed looks in remarkably good condition for this date and freight movements in connection with the MG car factory continued for many years after passenger services were withdrawn. (F.W. Shuttleworth Collection)

South of Radley, the Abingdon branch line is seen in the foreground, running alongside the main line, as BR-built 'Castle' class 4-6-0 No 7029, 'Clun Castle', heads towards Didcot with an enthusiasts' special on 4th October 1975. (Audie Baker/Kidderminster Railway Museum)

The line was worked throughout its life as 'one engine in steam'. Abingdon also had a regular engine that was serviced, coaled and watered there and resided in the engine shed overnight. Early in 1954 the shed was closed and all the engines used on the line thereafter worked out of Oxford shed, with a push-pull coach that was left at Radley overnight but taken once a week to Oxford for cleaning and maintenance.

The passenger service at this time was also curtailed with most afternoon journeys removed from the timetable. For the next nine years the Abingdon branch led an uneventful life until British Railways' good housekeeping measures led to the withdrawal of the passenger service on 9th September 1963.

Remarkably the branch stayed open for another 21 years as a freight-only line, serving the MG car plant and a number of Abingdon coal merchants. After the MG works closed in 1979 a modest service remained with an 08 diesel shunter working the odd trip into the coal yard. This eventually became uneconomical and the line closed completely in June 1984.

Today nothing of the Abingdon branch line has survived apart from sections of the trackbed used as a cycleway and footpath. This runs from Abingdon Junction, between the expanses of water that were gravel pits, and alongside parts of Barton Lane. At the Abingdon end there are no remains of the station and a Waitrose supermarket now occupies the site. The goods yard has succumbed to various commercial and domestic housing developments.

The MG car plant has long gone and the site has now become a McDonalds restaurant and a police station. In Cemetery Road, however, a vestige of the past still stands as the MG Owners and Members Club.

The Abingdon branch line was in some respects a special railway. It was the first branch line to be built in the area and although having a route length of just 2½ miles and a journey time of only 10 minutes between Abingdon and Radley – it survived for 128 years.

It is now just a memory.

8
Yarnton to Fairford

An undated view of Fairford station, showing its single platform with signal box, GWR wooden signal post and gas lights. (J. Tarrant/Kidderminster Railway Museum)

At 22¼ miles the line between Yarnton Junction and Fairford was the longest branch line in Oxfordshire – even taking into account the four miles or so within the county of Gloucestershire. The line in fact was created in two stages, the first of which was Oxford to Witney in 1861, followed by the 14-mile section from Fairford to Witney in 1873.

Some years prior to this a number of schemes were proposed to link Witney with the outside world, particularly from the larger established railway companies competing for territory. None of these schemes amounted to anything but because of a cooling of relations between the Oxford, Worcester & Wolverhampton Railway (OW&WR) and the Great Western Railway (GWR) a way forward was proposed at a public

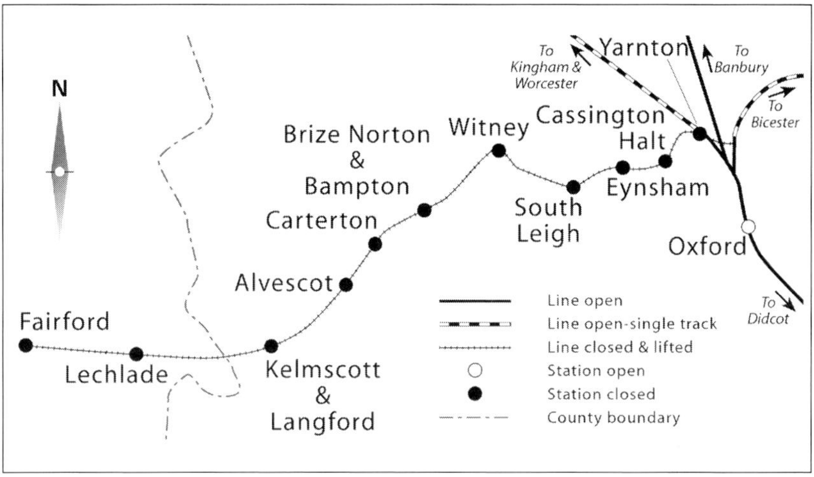

meeting held in Witney on 23rd December 1858. Here a decision was made by the great and good of Witney to form an independent Witney Railway (WR) to build a line from the town to a junction with the OW&WR at Yarnton.

No time was wasted and the following year the Witney Railway Bill, in the face of fierce objection from the GWR, received Royal Assent on 1st August 1859. Powers were also obtained for the OW&WR to operate the line on behalf of the WR over the first ten years in return for 50% of the gross receipts. However, following various ownership changes the agreement was subsequently amended so that the day-to-day running of the railway would pass to the West Midland Railway (WMR) to provide all necessary operational equipment and crews.

Construction began on 19th May 1860 and with no significant engineering obstacles in the way, work was completed very quickly. The line was laid to standard gauge and two intermediate stations, between Yarnton and Witney, were provided at Eynsham and South Leigh.

At 2 pm on a rainy Wednesday, 13th November 1861, to the sounds of a brass band and bells ringing out from the local church, a large gathering of people witnessed the first passenger train to arrive at the single-platform Witney station.

The following day a regular passenger timetable commenced with four services departing from Witney to Oxford each weekday. Goods facilities at Witney were provided the following year and this soon became well utilised by the local mill owners, with blanket trade being shipped out of the town and substantial wagonloads of coal, timber and other goods being brought in.

For the next twelve years the little branch line prospered and so did the town of Witney. However, during that time another independent railway, the East Gloucestershire Railway (EGR), made plans to serve Witney. The EGR obtained powers on 29th July 1864 to build a line from Cheltenham to Faringdon with a branch line to Witney but soon after construction started (from Cheltenham) in 1866 it became apparent that with the funds available it was unlikely that the EGR could complete the railway end-to-end as originally planned.

It was decided therefore that the line from Fairford to Witney could be built within the existing budget and in May 1869 work started on this part of the line. As work progressed the EGR found itself in similar operational circumstances to the Witney Railway with no locomotives or rolling stock in its ownership. Having little choice, the EGR directors signed an agreement with the GWR to operate the railway in exchange for 50% of the gross revenue received.

On 15th January 1873 the EGR line from Fairford was opened to the public to a new joint station at Witney with intermediate stations at Lechlade, Alvescot and Bampton. The original Witney station was subsequently expanded to become an extensive goods yard and depot.

The two independent companies could now provide a through service from Fairford to Oxford and this they did, with four return trips per day, remaining unchanged until 1890. This was the year in which the GWR made a bid to take over both the Witney and East Gloucestershire Railway companies and following recommendations from their respective directors, the shareholders of both companies sold their investments to the GWR and the transfer took place on 1st July 1890.

From hereon the GWR ran the branch line under its standard operational practice, installing signalling improvements and new signal boxes during 1892. As a consequence the train services increased to seven trains per weekday (Monday to Saturday) between Oxford and Witney, five of which ran though to Fairford. Seven years later a Sunday service, comprising one

A photograph of one of the original station name boards at Witney, c1965, and given the passage of time it has survived in remarkably good condition. (F.W. Shuttleworth Collection)

return trip between Oxford and Fairford, was introduced. The timetable then remained relatively unchanged until after the First World War when a Saturday-only midday trip between Oxford and Witney was added.

In 1906 the GWR introduced its famous Automatic Train Control (ATC) to this branch line. This provided an audible system of bells and sirens to warn drivers at each Distant signal if the road was clear – a bell sounded for clear and a siren for danger. Although the system was created for double-track working the GWR wished to try it on single-track branch lines. After modifying the locomotives with dual 'Up' and 'Down' electric circuits the system worked successfully on the Fairford branch, resulting in all of the line's Distant signals being removed. This remained as a unique operational feature throughout the railway's life.

The GWR continued to invest in the Fairford branch and in a bid to attract more custom to the line it opened Kelmscott & Langford station in 1907, followed by Cassington Halt in 1936.

As the Second World War got underway the railway became a hive of activity and because of wartime requirements to serve the RAF airfields at Brize Norton, Fairford and Broadwell, together with Army camps established at Eynsham and Witney, new passing loops were installed at Lechlade and Eynsham, and additional sidings laid at Fairford. In 1944 another station was built to serve Brize Norton. Located between Bampton and Alvescot stations it was named Carterton and during the closing years of the war it became one of the busiest stations on the railway.

In keeping with the rest of the nation's railway system, the Fairford branch faced the uncertainty associated with nationalisation but because of the improvements made to the line during hostilities it was perhaps better placed than most branch lines.

As it turned out, the railway continued almost unchanged right up to closure but throughout its life the Witney–Oxford section provided most of the passenger and goods revenue. The EGR line between Witney and Fairford was closed to all services on Monday, 18th June 1962 and the last timetabled passenger train to operate over the Fairford branch departed from Fairford to Oxford on Saturday, 16th June 1962.

Witney station on 25th July 1959 as '5700' class 0-6-0PT No 9654 takes on water whilst working an Oxford to Fairford train. At the other platform also taking on water is a train working from Fairford to Oxford.

A good view of Fairford's locomotive shed, c1960, with ex-GWR '1400' class 0-4-2T No 1435 in residence. To the right is a grounded horse-box, presumably used as a store.

For the next two years the Fairford–Witney part of the line yielded to nature, until the last quarter of 1964 when a private scrap merchant was authorised to remove the track. By early 1965 they had reached Witney and the town's original station became a terminus for the second time in 92 years.

Although the Beeching axe was raised over the remaining part of the branch line, goods trains continued to work out of Witney until 1970 when the line's leading customer, the Witney Blanket Co, was eventually forced to ship its products by road. Witney's EGR-built 'through' station was demolished in 1969 and the very last train, a BR special 'The Witney Wanderer', operated as far as Witney Junction on Saturday, 31st October 1970, followed by complete closure on Monday, 2nd November 1970.

Taking an imaginary trip over the line today, our train of three coaches would depart from Oxford station's north 'Down' bay platform, probably behind one of the 35xx Metropolitan 2-4-0 tanks, to run the first 3¾ miles to Yarnton. The station here, built by the OW&WR, had two platforms with a basic wooden station building on the north platform and a small corrugated-iron shelter on the opposite platform. Although a large nine-road

Ex-GWR Collett 'Dukedog' class 4-4-0 No 9015 is seen here shunting at Witney Goods station on the line to the original terminus station. The photograph was taken from the 6.10 pm Fairford to Oxford, passing Witney Junction, 8th June 1954. (Jeff Wood/Kidderminster Railway Museum)

marshalling yard and turntable were built during the Second World War there was no goods shed or transhipment facilities. Today nothing remains of Yarnton station or yard.

Immediately beyond the station is Yarnton Junction where the train leaves the main line and heads south-west onto the Fairford branch and, after just over one mile, the first station is reached – Cassington Halt. The halt was a GWR addition and consisted of a single concrete platform and small wooden shelter. Nothing remains of the station site now but the stone over-bridge carrying the A40 is still there, having undergone some significant refurbishment during 2004.

Crossing the River Evenlode on a large iron plate girder bridge the line heads towards Eynsham station, which was situated just south of the village. The station had a stone-built platform and wooden station building, together with a GWR signal cabin. The station site is now occupied by an industrial estate but its platform was removed and relocated to the Didcot Railway Centre. The iron bridge over the River Evenlode is still in situ and used to carry a private road.

A view of Eynsham station c1966 after passenger and goods services had been withdrawn. Eynsham differed in its construction; rather than being brick-built it was a wooden structure with a slate roof. It is unclear whether or not the corrugated shed was added before or after closure. (Author's Collection)

At 5½ miles from Yarnton, after first passing the crossing keeper's cottage and going over the level crossing, South Leigh station is reached. The station had a single platform, with a typical Witney Railway designed station building, cattle dock and parcels shed. A bungalow built in the 1990s now occupies the station site but the crossing keeper's house survives almost unaltered as a private dwelling.

Between South Leigh and Witney the line passes beneath a large stone-built road bridge known locally as the 'Ballaso'. It was so named after the nearby quarry from which the Witney Railway extracted ballast during the railway's construction. The bridge stands today as a reminder of the area's railway heritage.

Just prior to Witney station the train passes Witney Junction, where the line divides, one running into Witney Goods station (the old terminus) while the 'main' line runs ahead to Witney

A view of the yard at Witney Goods station, which was the original Witney passenger station before the Fairford section opened. Goods wagons are visible in the sidings, 31st March 1962. (G.E.S. Parker/Kidderminster Railway Museum)

After closure to passengers the waiting shelter at Witney is looking the worse for wear, c1965. (F.W. Shuttleworth Collection)

An undated view of Brize Norton & Bampton station, showing the double platforms that were provided at some of the stations on this single line branch. The station had a modest brick station building and a platform-mounted signal box. (J. Tarrant/Kidderminster Railway Museum)

(EGR) station. Here were two stone-built platforms and a station building in typical EGR style, with a later GWR 'pagoda' shelter and signal box. The other platform was furnished with a small timber-built shelter.

Today the combined site of both Witney stations is occupied by a large industrial estate and supermarket. Although the stationmaster's house and remnants of the goods shed have survived, the railway trackbed has been removed or severed by various road schemes and the Witney bypass.

After Witney the train ambles through undulating countryside for the next 3¾ miles before arriving at Brize Norton & Bampton. The station had two platforms and an EGR stone-built main building, GWR signal cabin and a small goods shed and cattle pens on the south side. Unfortunately, nothing remains of Bampton station site after it was taken over by the developers of an industrial estate.

Leaving Bampton the railway crossed two of Brize Norton airfield's main taxiways, giving rise to one of the most unusual and unique traffic management activities in the country, where Brize Norton's control tower and Bampton signal box co-ordinated the movement of aircraft across the taxiway level crossings! This arrangement ceased, however, when the railway closed and Brize Norton extended the airfield boundaries to enclose the former trackbed.

After three minutes' running time the train arrives at Carterton, the last station to be built on the line. It was a modest station with two platforms and a main building constructed from pre-cast concrete sections. Although the GWR provided a signal box there were no sidings or goods shed. Today the station building survives and is in commercial use. The signal box remained until 1980 when it was relocated to the Swindon & Cricklade Railway where it was dismantled to provide parts for the railway's other signal boxes.

The next stop down the line is at Alvescot, almost 14 miles from Yarnton. This was another EGR-design station, with a

Although there is no date recorded for this picture of Alvescot, judging by the sack trucks and wheelbarrows on the platform the station is still open. A brick and slate roof station building and corrugated iron 'pagoda' style storeroom is an interesting combination. (J. Tarrant/Kidderminster Railway Museum)

A view of Fairford station on 19th October 1957, looking towards the goods yard and the end of the line. The goods shed can be seen in the background with the platform mounted signal box and station building. (Author's Collection)

Looking very sad and neglected, this was the scene at Fairford station in 1965 after the line had been closed and lifted. (Author's Collection)

single platform that was occupied by a main building, which was unusually built from brick. The station site is now in use as a local transport depot.

Another short run and our train enters Kelmscott & Langford station. Built by the GWR, it had goods sidings, a cattle dock and a single brick-built platform on which stood a typical 'pagoda' shelter – but enlarged to provide the main station building facilities. At the time of writing the site has not been developed and the platform and cattle dock remain but are gradually becoming overgrown.

Another 2¼ miles and the train rolls into Lechlade station, one which had all the attributes of a EGR station: stone-built platform, main building and signal box, together with sidings, goods shed and cattle dock. As with Kelmscott & Langford the station site has not been subject to modern development but it remains, devoid of any structures.

The last leg of our journey to Fairford takes all of six minutes to the terminus station, which is, however, more than a mile from the town. The facilities at Fairford comprised the EGR-designed stone-built station, platform and signal box. The station had a large goods shed and sidings, cattle dock, GWR single-road wooden engine shed and a turntable. Interestingly for a branch line and good for the enginemen, the turntable allowed locomotives to always run chimney-first out of Fairford.

The station site now is taken up entirely by factory premises but the bridge that carried the A417 Cirencester–Faringdon road over the railway, as it once entered the station, is still in use.

Similar to other closed branch lines in the country the Fairford branch has been the subject of well-meaning groups who have over the years articulated proposals to reopen all or part of the line. As late as 2002 a survey was carried out to establish the feasibility of such schemes and it was determined that in view of the former trackbed being occupied by a range of commercial developments, housing estates and various major road schemes, any proposals to reinstate the railway would be economically unsustainable and prohibitively expensive.

A lost railway indeed.

9
Kidlington to Blenheim & Woodstock

Blenheim & Woodstock station on 13th June 1931 with ex-GWR '517' class 0-4-2T No 830 arriving with the 4 pm Saturdays only autocoach from Oxford. The locomotive was built at Wolverhampton in 1873 and withdrawn from service in January 1936. (A.W. Croughton/Kidderminster Railway Museum)

Three and a half miles west of the GWR's Oxford to Birmingham main line at Kidlington lay the ancient borough of Woodstock and the vast expanse of Blenheim Palace, home to the Dukes of Marlborough and birthplace of Winston Spencer Churchill.

When Churchill was born, on 30th November 1874, Woodstock was still isolated from the expanding railway network. The main line had been opened in 1850 and 40 years were to pass before the railway reached Woodstock.

Even so, the line was not promoted by any of the major railway companies. It was to become a private venture funded by His Grace George Charles, 8th Duke of Marlborough, with

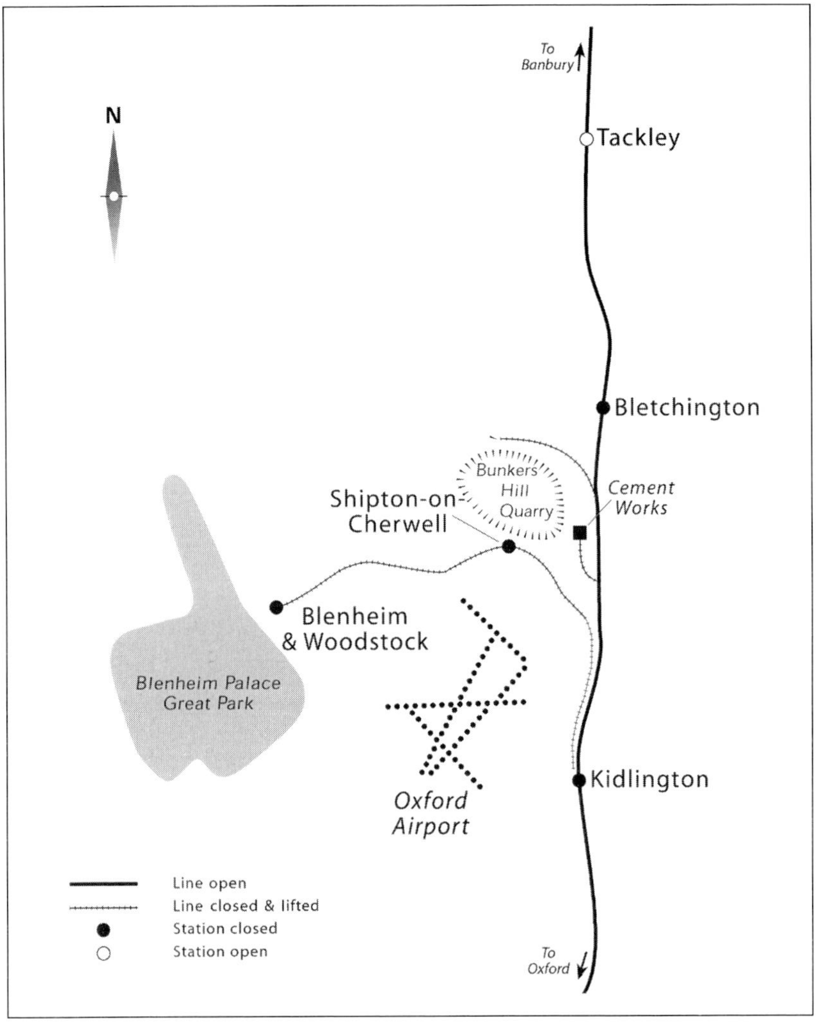

the Railway Act of 25th September 1886 that incorporated the Woodstock Railway Company (WRC).

The Act authorised the company to raise £10,000 capital and to build a railway from a junction with the Great Western Railway, near to Shipton-on-Cherwell, to Woodstock, terminating on the eastern side of the Oxford–Woodstock road almost opposite Hensington Gate, one of the main entrances to Blenheim.

Construction of the 3½-mile branch line was commenced in April 1888 by the railway's appointed contractors, Messrs Lucas & Aird, the work taking just over two years to complete. As with many locally promoted branch lines at this time, the staffing and operational equipment was invariably provided by an established railway company. In this case the WRC had entered into an agreement with the GWR to operate the branch on their behalf.

The branch was officially opened on 19th May 1890; the first train started its run from Oxford station at 6 am with the Oxford stationmaster on board. After leaving Kidlington the train travelled north over new metals that were laid parallel with the Oxford–Birmingham main line for a mile before turning west, over the Oxford Canal, towards Shipton-on-Cherwell. The train arrived in Woodstock to be met by a large gathering of townsfolk and most of the local children, who were not only given a day off from school but also a free breakfast, arranged by the Mayor of Woodstock, and a free trip on the train to Kidlington and back.

The next day a regular timetable of four return trains each weekday was introduced between Woodstock and the newly constructed platform at Kidlington station, which prior to the branch being opened was known as Woodstock Road station.

The timetable continued mostly unchanged for the next seven years when, in 1897, the GWR made a successful bid to amalgamate the WRC within its network.

During the early years of the railway the Duke of Marlborough travelled frequently on the line, making use of a private first class carriage usually attached to a service train. In 1896 Queen Victoria made an official visit to Blenheim Palace, her train travelling on the branch line behind a '517' class 0-4-2T locomotive, No 1473, which on the day of the Queen's visit was officially named *Fair Rosamund*. This locomotive was built at Wolverhampton in 1883, seven years before the Woodstock branch opened, and thereafter it remained as the Woodstock railway's principal motive power for 45 years, during which time the locals knew her as 'Rosie'.

Facilities at Blenheim & Woodstock station were quite comprehensive for a branch line terminus and well capable of handling the VIP visitors to Blenheim Palace. There was modest but regular goods traffic, as well as farmers' produce and cattle movements and frequent wagonloads of coal delivered to a number of Woodstock's coal merchants, some of whom operated their own brightly painted Private Owner wagons. The Pullen Glove Factory also had its own siding from which it shipped out its famous 'Woodstock Gloves'.

The large L-shaped station building had a single platform and the yard area was laid out with a goods shed and hand-operated crane, together with a separate loading dock and cattle dock. There was also a single-road engine shed but this was in fact closed and dismantled in 1926, and the resident locomotive was then required to be rostered out of Oxford shed.

Although a curiously tall signal cabin controlled Woodstock's yard until 1926, when lever frames replaced it, there was no block signalling since the line was worked by 'Train Staff One Engine in Steam at a time, or two coupled together'.

In 1929 an intermediate station was introduced on the line, Shipton-on-Cherwell Halt, one of 26 or so new halts built that year by the GWR in order to help stimulate branch line passenger traffic. The halt was situated on the embankment near to the bridge that carried the railway over the A423 trunk road

Apart from a halt on the branch line, Shipton-on-Cherwell also had a large cement works and its own railway system. This picture, taken on 4th November 1961, shows 1921-built Bagnall (build No 2178) 0-4-0ST standing at the loco shed situated on the cement works. (L.W. Perkins/ W. Wycherley/Kidderminster Railway Museum)

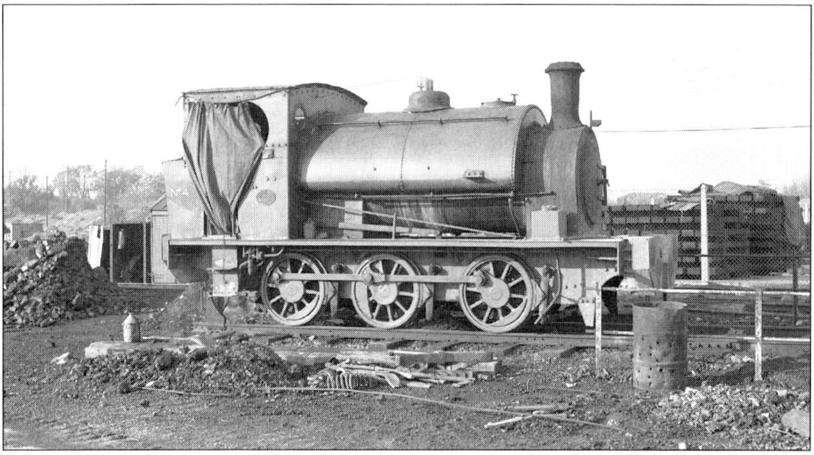

Standing at what appears to be the 'coaling' area at Shipton-on-Cherwell cement works on 4th November 1961 is 1929-built Hunslet 0-6-0ST, No 4. The build number is recorded as 1643 but it could be number 1649. (L.W. Perkins/W. Wycherley/Kidderminster Railway Museum)

(now the A4260). Passenger facilities were basic, however, with a diminutive platform, built entirely from sleepers, just large enough to accommodate a small wooden shelter.

During April 1950 Blenheim Palace threw open its doors to the general public but each year thereafter visitors to Blenheim arriving by train diminished. By this time, the service had been cut from ten return trips to seven trips per weekday, worked by a locomotive and autocoach. There was no Sunday service which could have attracted the weekend visitor to Blenheim. As it was, visitors arrived by motor coach in their hundreds!

In his book *The Woodstock Branch*, Richard Lindgard tells of a regular passenger who 'remembers how the driver often used to take pot shots at rabbits and hares, with lumps of coal. If by any chance he succeeded in hitting one he would stop the train, climb down from the engine and "bag" his supper for that evening'.

This could easily have given the idea to the writer of the film *The Titfield Thunderbolt* for a cameo scene where the locomotive driver shoots a pheasant from the footplate and stops the train to collect it, much to the annoyance of the passengers!

The film told the story of a group of townspeople of 'Titfield' who purchased the local branch line to 'Mallingford' from British

Railways to operate their own service. When a local rival bus company decided to sabotage the engine, a 14xx tank, two of the main characters, played by Stanley Holloway and Hugh Griffith, in a somewhat drunken state set out to 'borrow' an engine (No 1462) from 'Mallingford' station (actually Bristol Temple Meads). They took the engine off the turntable and proceeded down the main streets, hoping to reach 'Titfield' by road! Although most of the film's location work was done on the closed GWR line from Limpley Stoke to Camerton, the street scenes at 'Mallingford' were filmed in Woodstock over three days, using a wooden mock-up of No 1462 attached to a commercial van chassis – complete with smoke and steam effects.

Released in March 1953, this was one of the first British films made in colour by Ealing Studios. It was also ironic that the film just preceded the closure of the Blenheim & Woodstock branch line in 1954. This followed a cut in the timetable to six trains per day and finally to four trains that were timed in such a way that there were no convenient connections at Kidlington. Typically, passengers from Woodstock had a two-hour wait for a train to Oxford, which in the end encouraged people onto Oxford Motor Services' No 42 bus service, running from Woodstock to Oxford via Kidlington. In the end the reduced and uncoordinated timetable, together with abstraction of fares from bus usage, brought about the closure of the line.

It was first announced that the line was to close in September 1953 and this gave rise to a considerable number of objections. There were various proposals on how the line might be kept open, including using diesel railcars or in fact a motor bus converted to run on rails, which could also stop at any point on the line, giving passengers the convenience of a bus service.

Whilst the arguments were considered and discussed there was a short deferment of six months. However, the Railway Executive were still focused on closure and set a date of 1st March 1954. The last train ran on Saturday, 27th February 1954, and with 150 or so tickets sold it departed Blenheim & Woodstock station strengthened to two autocoaches, which were required for the additional load, and motive power was provided by 14xx 2-4-0T locomotive No 1420. As usual on these occasions, a large crowd gathered on the station platform to witness the spectacle as another of the country's branch lines met its fate and closed forever.

Suitably adorned with a chalk face, ex-GWR '1400' class 0-4-2T No 1420 stands at Blenheim & Woodstock station on the last day of services on 27th February 1954. It is puzzling to see a group of smiling faces on the last day of their train service. (R.S. Carpenter)

Had the railway survived until 1965 I believe it would have played a major part in the funeral arrangements for Sir Winston Churchill, returning him by train to his birthplace and burial at the village church of Bladon, situated on the edge of Blenheim Park.

As it was, the authorities were obliged to run the funeral train to the nearest main line station to Blenheim, Hanborough Halt, which was located on the Oxfordshire, Worcester & Wolverhampton Railway. There was a logistical problem here, though, because the access road to the halt was on the Up side. British Railways found a solution by installing a crossover from the Down line at that point, thereby providing an appropriate and fitting conclusion to the solemn journey.

The journey to Bladon began at Waterloo where the train, awaiting at platform 11, consisted of Bulleid Pacific 34051, *Sir Winston Churchill*, (crewed by Driver A.W. Hurley and 22-year-old fireman J.C. Lester), Pullman brake car 208, baggage luggage van S2464 (carrying the coffin), Pullman cars *Carina, Lydia, Perseus* and Pullman brake car *Isle of Thanet*. The train left

Had the Blenheim & Woodstock branch remained open until 30th January 1965, there is little doubt that the funeral train for Sir Winston Churchill would have operated over the Woodstock branch. As it was, the train worked to Hanborough station, which was then the nearest station to Blenheim. This photograph shows the train, on its return journey behind 'Western' hydraulic No D1015 'Western Champion', through a crowded Oxford station. (F.W. Shuttleworth)

Waterloo at 1328 hrs and arrived at Hanborough at 1523 hrs. Following the ceremony the Bulleid was taken off and returned to Nine Elms and the train returned to Paddington behind diesel hydraulic D1015, *Western Champion*.

Later that same year, van No S2464 was purchased by an American businessman who exported it to California to form part of an imaginary English railway station at a resort hotel in Los Angeles. Since it became surplus to requirements a few years ago its owners, the Los Angeles City of Industry, arranged to donate the van to the Swanage Railway where, given the appropriate funding, it will be restored to working order.

Following closure of the Woodstock branch in 1954, almost four years were to pass before the track was finally lifted on 26th January 1958. At the same time, Young's Garages purchased Blenheim & Woodstock station building and converted it into a car showroom with the station frontage transformed into a petrol forecourt.

Today the station building still survives as a car showroom but without the petrol franchise. As a reminder of its railway

Blenheim & Woodstock station frontage in 1972 after it had been taken over by Young's Garages and converted to a petrol station. It is interesting to note that the most expensive petrol on sale is 5 star Esso Extra at 37p per gallon! (Author's Collection)

past, the rear of the building (railway side) still has a small section of the platform awning in place and although there is a remnant of track hidden in the undergrowth, the remainder of the station site and goods yard is now occupied by a roofing company/storage facility.

Parts of the old trackbed are still intact (but overgrown) on the approach to Woodstock, alongside Hensington Road and just south of Shipton Slade Farm, but any remnants of Shipton-on-Cherwell Halt have long since gone and the once substantial over-bridge that took the railway over the A4260 is now but a memory. From here, however, the trackbed can be picked up again in parts, making a very enjoyable saunter, heading eastwards, before meeting the railway bridge over the Oxfordshire Canal, which still carries trains on the main line, and the point at which the branch line would have swung south towards Kidlington.

To the casual walker, unaware of its past, this is just a pleasant byway but to the railway enthusiast it provides a precious reminder of this lost railway.

10
Kings Sutton to Kingham

Kingham station on 23rd April 1962, looking west, with the main through lines in the foreground. Standing in the 'Banbury' branch platform is ex-GWR '5101' class 2-6-2T No 4101 having just arrived with the 2.30 pm Cheltenham (St James) to Chipping Norton. In the distance can be seen the over-bridge that carried the direct 'avoiding' line to Cheltenham. (Jeff Wood/Kidderminster Railway Museum)

It could be said that had it not been for the persistence of two gentlemen of Chipping Norton, William Bliss (in particular), the owner of the Bliss Tweed Mill, and Robert Hitchman of Hitchman's Brewery, a line connecting Chipping Norton to the then rapidly expanding railway network might not have been built. From this humble beginning the railway developed into the 47-mile-long direct route between Banbury and Cheltenham Spa. This chapter, however, will discuss mainly the part of the line that ran through Oxfordshire – Kings Sutton to Kingham.

During September 1847, whilst the Oxford, Worcester & Wolverhampton Railway (OW&WR) was struggling with constructing its own main line, William Bliss wrote to the

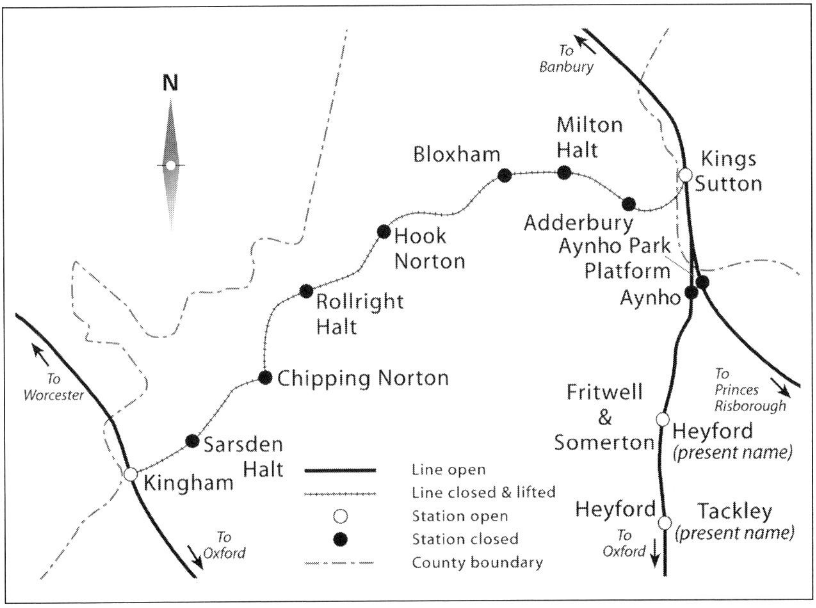

OW&WR board of directors in order to persuade them of the benefits of building their railway to include Chipping Norton, which Bliss looked upon as the most significant town between Oxford and Evesham. In his letter he also set out the considerable tonnage of goods and materials exported from Chipping Norton each year, all of which would likely transfer to the railway should the line be provided. Because Bliss already had in mind plans to convert his water-driven mills to steam power, the expectation of copious supplies of cheap coal being brought in by rail was also clearly on his agenda.

The OW&WR directors informed Bliss that they had considered the possibility of a station in or near Chipping Norton but remained convinced that the line of railway and the station sites already decided upon met the requirements of the area they were going to serve.

The great and good of Chipping Norton, however, were not about to give in and over the following four years various correspondence was dispatched to the OW&WR but it was to no avail. On 4th June 1853 the OW&WR opened its line from Wolvercot Junction to Evesham, bypassing Chipping Norton by some four miles.

That same year William Bliss led a delegation from Chipping Norton to make a final request to the OW&WR for a station to be provided at Bledington for the convenience of Chipping Norton folk. The request was summarily refused.

This left William Bliss with a dilemma – give in or champion a plan to build a railway independently. In fact the intransigence of the OW&WR made Bliss even more determined and with the support of Robert Hitchman and others he pressed ahead with a proposal for a branch line to link with the OW&WR.

They were then blessed with good fortune when an already successful railway builder, Sir Morton Peto, understanding the enthusiasm of fellow Baptist William Bliss, offered to build the railway to Chipping Norton and, using his own money, provided more than half the estimated £26,000 construction costs. Bliss, Hitchman and a number of interested townsfolk eagerly funded the shortfall.

And so, in 1854, the Chipping Norton Railway Company was formed and following the usual legal requirements the railway was authorised to build a 4½-mile standard gauge (4′ 8½″) branch line from Chipping Norton to a junction with the OW&WR's line at a point midway between Bledington and Kingham, to be known as 'Chipping Norton Junction', with one intermediate station sited near Churchill but named Sarsden Halt. Although Sarsden village was over a mile away the halt was named as a concession to one of the railway's promoters, James Haughton Langston of Sarsden House, who owned most of the land upon which the branch line was built. It was 1909 before Chipping Norton Junction took on its current and well-known name of Kingham.

Work started on the branch in September 1854 and (unheard of in railway construction at the time) was finished within its budget of £26,000. In May 1855 the engineering works were complete and following the formalities of the Board of Trade Railway Inspectorate a grand opening ceremony took place on Friday, 10th August 1855. A working agreement had been made with the OW&WR to provide motive power and stock in exchange for 50% of the gross revenue. A Robert Stephenson & Co 2-2-2 well tank, one of two such engines to work the line in its early years, hauled the first train. The following Monday, a weekday-only service commenced with three return trains per day.

The opening day was such an occasion that the Lord Mayor of Chipping Norton laid on a lavish banquet at the town hall and, although a modest three courses, there were 27 items to choose from! It ended a day of celebration for a little branch line that was eventually to form part of a much longer route that would enable the townsfolk of Chipping Norton to venture far and wide.

However, just over 32 years were to pass before the final link was made to extend the line eastwards to Kings Sutton and on to Banbury. During that time priority was given to moving the line in the direction of Cheltenham. The Chipping Norton Junction to Bourton on the Water section was the first to open, on 1st March 1862. By 1881 a connection was made at Cheltenham and on 1st June of that year a through service from Cheltenham to Oxford became operational.

During these interim years the profitable Chipping Norton branch line was taken over by the OW&WR in 1859 and subsequently in 1863 it too amalgamated with the mighty Great Western Railway.

Chipping Norton to Kings Sutton was the last section of the grand 'Banbury & Cheltenham Direct Railway' and the approval was given in 1874 for the work to proceed in accordance with plans submitted by Edward Wilson, which included stations at Adderbury, Bloxham, Hook Norton and a halt provided at Rollright. Although construction started in 1875 all work was brought to a standstill in 1878 due to a national economic crisis and it was late 1879 before work recommenced.

Significant engineering features also defined this part of the railway. Heading towards Kings Sutton, immediately after leaving Chipping Norton station, a tunnel of 750 yards was required to penetrate the hillside. A second 418-yard tunnel, east of Rollright, was followed by two magnificent 90-ft-high viaducts spanning the valley on the approach to Hook Norton station. The viaducts, of five and eight spans respectively, were of steel girder construction supported on stone-built piers and this took several hundred navvies all of four years to complete. Hook Norton's alehouses must have been interesting places during that time!

Hook Norton, however, was familiar with hard-working men because of the growth of ironstone mines in the area and associated narrow gauge (and standard gauge) lines that were built to serve them. But more of this in Chapter 11.

Ex-GWR '4800' class 0-4-2T No 4858 at Adderbury station c1939 with a stopping train from Banbury to Kingham. Two auto coaches are behind the engine and the signal box is visible behind the last coach. (J.B. Phillipson/Kidderminster Railway Museum)

Without any great ceremony this final part of the railway was officially opened on 6th April 1887, enabling trains to travel from the Birmingham & Oxford line at Kings Sutton to Cheltenham, albeit, for a few years, requiring reversals at Chipping Norton Junction. In 1906 this problem was overcome when the Kingham Avoiding Line was introduced to bypass the junction, utilising a steel girder bridge spanning the OW&WR tracks, which finally created the 'direct' railway. This action eliminated most of the reversing movements required at the junction and freed up the line to additional through freight workings. It also made possible a weekday-only cross-country express service from Newcastle-upon-Tyne to Barry and Swansea – the 'Ports to Ports Express'.

In 1922 *Bradshaw's Guide* showed that Chipping Norton enjoyed a weekday (Monday to Saturday) service of twelve trains per day to Kingham and eleven return workings, with Chipping Norton to Banbury trains consisting of six return workings each weekday.

By 1939 a decline in service began to show and the famous 'Ports to Ports Express' had been withdrawn from the direct line.

Although the branch became well utilised during the Second World War, passenger numbers continued to diminish with increased pressure from competing local bus services. The situation did not improve following nationalisation in 1948 and this brought early closure to passengers for Adderbury station, Milton Halt, Bloxham station and Hook Norton station on 4th June 1951.

In 1962 Beeching recommended withdrawal of passenger services on the remaining parts of the line. The first to go was the section between Kingham and Cheltenham on 15th October 1962, followed two months later by the original part of the branch, from Kingham to Chipping Norton, officially closing on 3rd December 1962, with the last passenger train operating on 1st December, hauled by BR 'Standard' 2-6-0 No 78001. Goods traffic continued at Bloxham and Hook Norton until 4th November 1963 and the following year Chipping Norton lost its goods traffic on 7th September 1964, the date at which the railway closed altogether. The exception to this was Adderbury station, which officially closed to all functions on 4th December 1967, having remained connected to the main line for conveyance of residual ironstone traffic from private sidings.

A post-war picture, c1946, taken at sidings on the Moreton-in-Marsh side of Kingham station, showing three rows of unidentified ex-WD 2-8-0 locomotives, with the exception of the front two, which bear the numbers 77012 and 77006. (L.W. Perkins/W. Wycherley/Kidderminster Railway Museum)

A photograph of Adderbury station from the veranda of a guard's van, 11th December 1954. (John Marshall/Kidderminster Railway Museum)

Taking our imaginary trip from Kings Sutton to Kingham, the line swings west off the main line to cross the River Cherwell and Oxford Canal bridges. It then passed beneath an overbridge carrying the B4100, Aynho Road, at a point that is now the Banbury Business Park, before reaching Adderbury station. The station was situated at the end of a long access road well below the A4260, Oxford Road, and consisted of two platforms, a brick-built station, a platform shelter and a signal box. There was also a substantial yard with a goods shed and private siding. Today the cuttings are filled and Station Yard Industrial Estate occupies the station site.

Leaving Adderbury under the A4260 bridge, the railway continues now as single line through West Adderbury and after 2 miles Milton Halt is passed with its single platform and 'pagoda' shelter, and after another mile the train rolls into Bloxham station. Bloxham consisted of a brick-built station with slate roof and wooden canopy, signal box, goods shed and cattle dock and a similar brick shelter on the Up platform. Unfortunately there are no recognisable remains of the railway that existed here.

Departing Bloxham the line proceeds beneath bridges spanning Milton Road and the A361 before heading south-west,

This is an undated view of Bloxham station showing the small station building, running-in board on the platform to the left and waiting shelter on the right and in the right foreground is the single line token catcher. (J. Tarrant/Kidderminster Railway Museum)

A photograph of Hook Norton station, unfortunately undated, showing the main station building, waiting shelter and goods shed in the right background. (J. Tarrant/Kidderminster Railway Museum)

past Milcombe and to the north of Wiggington, for 4½ miles to Hook Norton station, which was in an elevated position and entered immediately after passing over a girder bridge spanning Station Road. The main building and shelter were both built of red brick with grey slate roofs and decorative awnings. There was a cattle dock, goods shed and yard with the ubiquitous coal wharf and, if your train was running late you could always take 'refreshment' at the Railway Hotel that was immediately behind the station entrance. Although the station site is now occupied by a housing development on Austin's Way, Station Road still exists and 'Railway Farm'.

Leaving Hook Norton the train proceeds onto the first of two 90-ft-high viaducts that carry the railway across the Swere Valley before heading south-west towards Rollright and the 418-yard Hook Norton Tunnel (also called Swerford Tunnel). Remarkably the stone piers to the viaducts still loom above the tree line and the railway cuttings are conserved and so is the tunnel but the portals are bricked-up at both ends.

After leaving Hook Norton Tunnel the line emerges just before Rollright Siding comes into view with a single siding

A wonderful view of Hook Norton Viaduct No 2, the southern of the two, both built from stone pillars supporting the iron girder rail-beds. In the distance, to the right of the bridge, can be seen the first bridge and Hook Norton station, 6th April 1960. (John Marshall/Kidderminster Railway Museum)

On 8th May 1954 a picture of the southern portal of Chipping Norton Tunnel taken just as a Banbury to Kingham pick-up goods, hauled by '2251' class 0-6-0 No 2202, exits to run into Chipping Norton station, which was just behind the photographer. (John Marshall/Kidderminster Railway Museum)

alongside the branch line, once equipped with a weighbridge, a small goods shed and loading gauges. Another ¼ mile and Rollright Halt is passed, with its Down side platform adorned with a GWR 'pagoda' shelter.

From Rollright the line leaves on a descending gradient for 3½ miles before diving into the blackness of Chipping Norton Tunnel, emerging almost immediately into Chipping Norton station, the highest station above sea level in Oxfordshire! It was the very first to be built on the branch and the largest station site between Kings Sutton and Kingham; its facilities included a substantial main building of red brick, grey slate roof and wooden awnings, alongside a platform-level signal box. The two platforms were connected by a decorative lattice iron footbridge and the generous sidings included a large brick-built goods shed, a coaling stage and long sidings, one of which led to the famous Bliss Tweed Mill.

Today Chipping Norton Tunnel is still intact but bricked-up at each end in such a way as to conserve any wildlife that takes refuge in the tunnel. Station Road remains and the station site is now Station Yard Industrial Estate whereas the mill, closed in 1980, is now a residential apartments development.

A general view of Chipping Norton station taken in the early 1950s, looking north towards the tunnel, which was just beyond the road bridge. The main station building and platform-built signal box with brick flat-roofed shelter on the Down side and ornate cast iron footbridge were all in good order at this time. (Joe Moss Collection)

Ex-GWR '4500' class 2-6-2T No 5514 stands by the signal box at Chipping Norton station, waiting the right away with a Banbury to Kingham service during the summer of 1958. (Author's Collection)

A c1907 view of Sarsden Halt, looking towards Kingham, with its single timber-built platform, running-in board, oil lamps and enamel advertising signs for Lipton's Tea. It also had a 'pagoda' style waiting shelter with 'damsel' at the door; brick-built signal box and crossing gates. (Tom Lane/Kidderminster Railway Museum)

Leaving Chipping Norton the line continues on a descending gradient and after 2 miles Sarsden Halt is reached. It consisted of a single wooden platform, with the usual corrugated iron 'pagoda' shelter, running parallel with a modest single-road goods siding. A signal box was situated at the Kingham end of the platform, immediately after the crossing-keeper's cottage and level crossing.

The name lives on as a group of houses in Churchill Mill is now known as 'Sarsden Halt' and the crossing-keeper's house still stands but is in private ownership. The original timetable board was saved and can now be seen on display at Winchcombe Railway Museum in Gloucestershire.

The last 2 miles of this journey to Kingham led to the East signal box where the branch line became a double-track junction, to provide Up and Down lines to the station and the lines to Cheltenham using the Avoiding Line over-bridge.

Entering Kingham station the Chipping Norton branch had its own platforms on the Up side. By the 1920s the station had

Ex-GWR '2301' class Dean Goods 0-6-0 No 2458 is seen outside Kingham shed with the tender of '2251' class 0-6-0 No 2295 in the right of the view. The picture was taken from a train leaving for Cheltenham (St James) on 23rd May 1952. (Jeff Wood/Kidderminster Railway Museum)

BR Standard class 2, 2-6-0 No 78001 stands outside Kingham shed with typical GWR signals and coaling stage in view, 11th May 1957. (W. Potter/ Kidderminster Railway Museum)

A view of Kingham station's main building c1965, when passenger trains on the branch lines had ceased and services were reserved for the main line only; there was an obvious air of dereliction at that time. (F.W. Shuttleworth Collection)

A view of Kingham station c1965 from the footbridge looking west over the platform that served the branch line to Chipping Norton and Banbury. The branch is seen swinging north as double track, providing Up and Down lines into the station but they are reduced to single track at Kingham East Junction. (F.W. Shuttleworth Collection)

At the west end of Kingham station Down platform, an interesting bracket signal was built with the arms amidships and counterweights raised to the top of the post, photographed c1965. This configuration provided locomotive drivers with a clear sighting through a road bridge that would have obscured a standard bracket signal. (F.W. Shuttleworth Collection)

achieved important junction status, complete with locomotive shed and turntable, and was enlarged only marginally during the Second World War when additional sidings were added.

Today Kingham station still survives, albeit a shadow of its glory days on the old OW&WR route, now better known as 'The Cotswold Line', and although parts of the line have been singled over the years, passenger numbers have increased steadily since 2000.

The little branch line, however, slumbers into history.

11
Connections with Banbury and the Ironstone Lines

On 25th March 1953 ex-GWR 'King' class 4-6-0 No 6016 'King Edward V' passes through Banbury General station with a Birkenhead to Paddington express. Ex-LNER 'N7' class 0-6-2T No 69621 stands in the adjacent platform with a local train to Woodford. (Brian Moone/Kidderminster Railway Museum)

Connections with Banbury are really just that, because the three railways that advanced from the east upon Banbury and the Great Western Railway lay for the most part in two adjacent counties, Northamptonshire and Buckinghamshire.

To the west of Banbury and wholly within Oxfordshire, ironstone deposits were being exploited to furnish the Industrial Revolution with one of its essential resources. Within the areas surrounding Wroxton, Adderbury, Bloxham and Hook Norton there were numerous ironstone pits that eventually had their own railway systems linked with the railway network where the iron ore or calcined products would be shipped out to various iron foundries in the industrial West Midlands and South Wales.

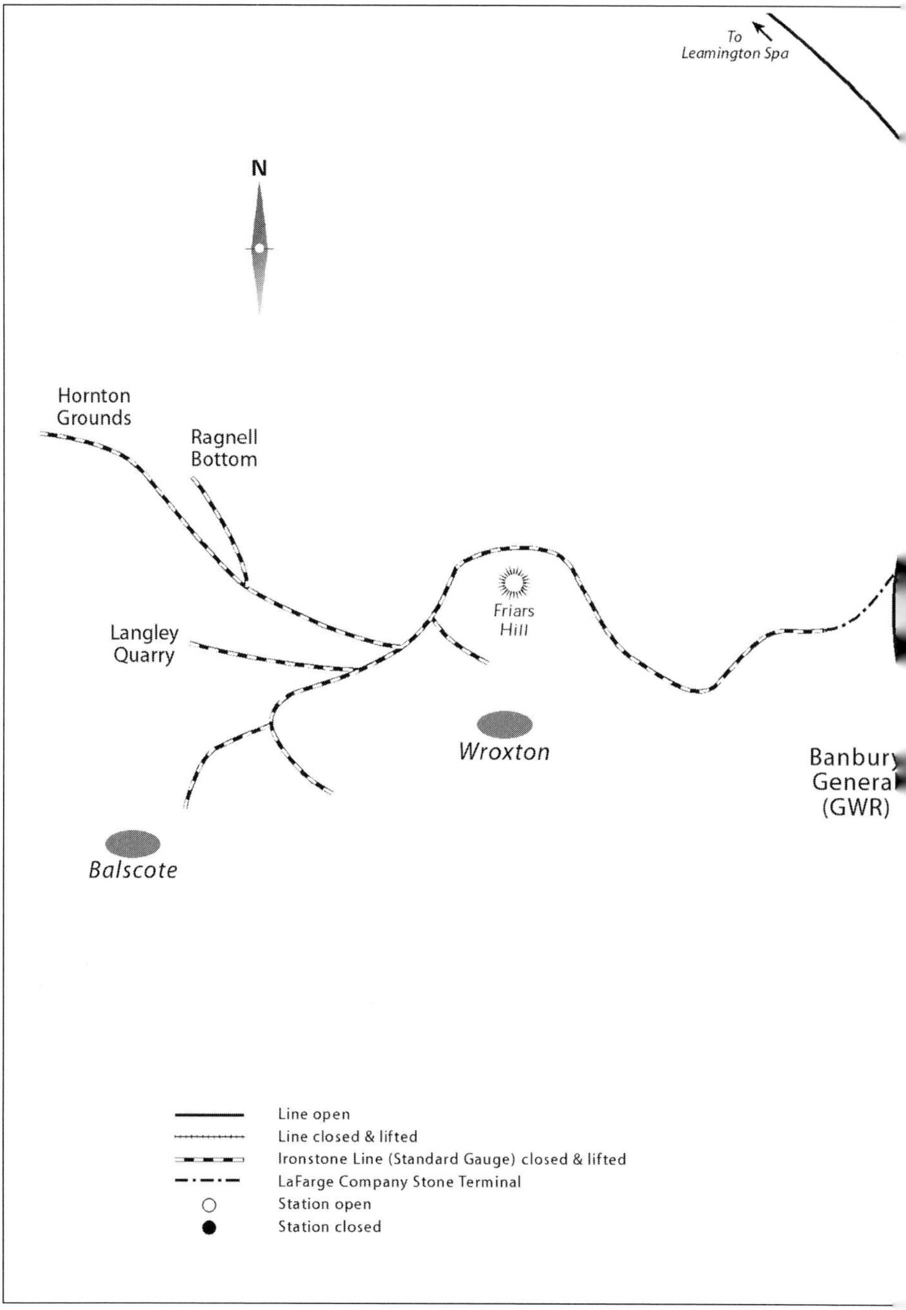
To
Leamington Spa
N
Hornton
Grounds
Ragnell
Bottom
Langley
Quarry
Friars
Hill
Wroxton
Balscote
Banbury
General
(GWR)
Line open
Line closed & lifted
Ironstone Line (Standard Gauge) closed & lifted
LaFarge Company Stone Terminal
Station open
Station closed

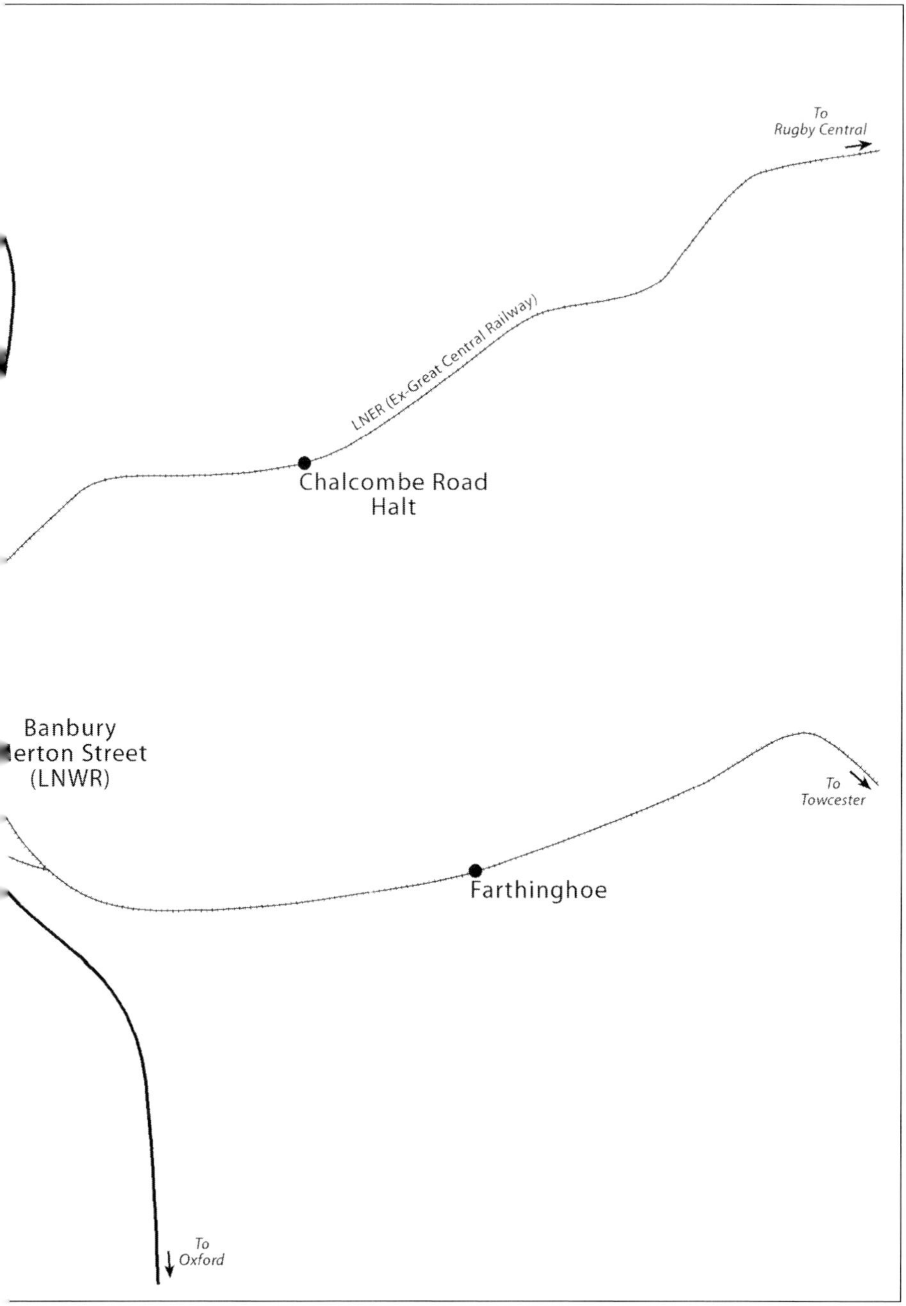
To
Rugby Central
LNER (Ex-Great Central Railway)
Chalcombe Road
Halt
Banbury
erton Street
(LNWR)
To
Towcester
Farthinghoe
To
Oxford

Banbury was celebrated for its livestock market but as the railways arrived, offering the scope for moving cattle and sheep far and wide, the scale of that market grew at an astonishing rate. Banbury soon became one of the most important junction stations in the country. In 1889 a permanent locomotive shed was built and following the connection with the Great Central in 1900 a much larger shed was opened on 24th August 1908 and substantial exchange sidings were laid, thereby establishing Banbury's strategic position on the national railway network.

The original Bridge Street station, comprising a single platform, opened on 2nd September 1850 as part of the GWR's broad gauge Oxford–Birmingham line. Four months earlier, however, and only a short distance away, Banbury Merton Street station had opened as a terminus for the Buckinghamshire Railway.

The arrival of the Buckinghamshire Railway in Banbury bridged the undefined sparsely populated area that lay between the London & Birmingham Railway line through Northamptonshire and the GWR's Oxford–Birmingham line. It also brought an end to the GWR's dominant position in this part of Oxfordshire.

It all began as the London & Birmingham Railway and the Grand Junction Railway joined forces to become the London & North Western Railway (LNWR). Now, this newly formed company was in a significant position to take on the GWR by being able to provide the considerable finance needed to bankroll a new railway and one that would serve both Banbury and Oxford.

Work on the Buckinghamshire Railway commenced in April 1847, from Bletchley to Claydon, where the separate routes to Banbury and Oxford would eventually diverge at Verney Junction. From here the Banbury branch had intermediate stations at Padbury, Buckingham, Fulwell & Westbury, Brackley and Farthinghoe. The line from Bletchley was laid as double track to Claydon and thereafter both lines (to Banbury and Oxford) were single throughout except for the stations with two platform faces, where both Up and Down tracks were laid.

On 1st May 1850, with great ceremony and in the presence of large crowds of people, bunting and a brass band, the first train left Banbury at 6.30 am to Bletchley, the earliest of four trains per weekday provided in the initial timetable. From this day the townspeople of Banbury had travel opportunities to destinations eastwards and an important alternative route to London.

Banbury Merton Street station frontage c1950, an interesting photograph showing what looks like a Morris 4-door saloon with two people checking a timetable board still with the LMS heading and a bicycle parked at the right hand side of the building. (R.K. Blencowe Archive)

Photographed from approximately the same position in July 2009, new developments have obscured any clue that a railway station stood here for over 100 years. (Author)

Farthinghoe was the first station on the LNWR line out of Banbury and served trains for both the Northampton and Bletchley lines. This view shows the station and station house and the short goods siding with livestock dock, 4th May 1959. (F.A. Blencowe/R.K. Blencowe Archive)

One of the stations on the Buckingham line, just on the cusp of Oxfordshire, is Fulwell & Westbury. Following complete closure on 2nd December 1963, the station house was purchased as a private dwelling and additional buildings were constructed to accommodate a car restoration business. This picture shows the station house with the new buildings behind and the remains of the platform, c1965. (Author's Collection)

A year earlier a scheme was proposed to link Banbury with Northampton and as a result the Northampton & Banbury Junction Railway (N&BJR) was formed. However, the promoters' efforts came to nothing at that time but they persevered with their endeavour and after the passage of 13 years the N&BJR was approved by Parliament and received Royal Assent on 28th July 1863.

As construction got underway on the first section from Blisworth to Towcester, the N&BJR seemed not content with its initial plans to reach Banbury. During the next three years the company placed various schemes before Parliament to extend its railway beyond Banbury. These schemes culminated in the Northampton & Banbury Junction Railway Act of 1866, which authorised the company to extend its line to Ross-on-Wye. Such was the scale of this scheme it was resolved that the company be renamed the 'Midland & South Wales Junction Railway'. However, within two months of opening the first section of the N&BJR to Towcester, on 30th April 1866, a banking crisis hit the country and the N&BJR's grand plans were set aside indefinitely.

Four years went by before authorisation was given to extend the line beyond Towcester and through to Banbury. On 14th July 1870 Royal Assent was granted to build the line from Towcester to the colourfully named Cockley Brake where a junction was to be created to connect with the Buckinghamshire Railway, over which running powers into Banbury had been obtained by the N&BJR.

The experienced railway contractor John Aird & Son was appointed to construct the 8-mile extension with intermediate stations at Wappenham and Helmdon. Work started in the early weeks of 1871 and progressed very quickly, and by the end of August the railway had been laid as far as Helmdon, a distance of 7½ miles from Towcester. The last section to Cockley Brake Junction was tackled at a more leisurely pace and eventually the completed line was opened to traffic on 1st June 1872, giving Banbury folk and the villages and settlements en route a means of reaching another large town within a matter of an hour or so, at a time when the only alternative was a horse and cart.

There was, however, one inconvenience – the LNWR never allowed the N&BJR running rights between Blisworth and Northampton and passengers were required to change trains at Blisworth. As a consequence any expectation of high passenger

Banbury Junction in October 1948 as an unidentified 'Hall' class 4-6-0 heads southbound towards Banbury with an empty stock train past the Great Central lines coming in from the right. The photograph was taken from the Junction signal box. (Millbrook House Ltd)

numbers or indeed robust freight traffic was short-lived since the prospect of undertaking a relatively short journey that required a change of trains in both directions was unappealing, and future loadings reflected this.

The timetable consisted of three weekdays-only trains each way from Banbury to Blisworth and remained unchanged until 1917 when wartime measures reduced the service to two Up and Down trains only. When hostilities ceased in 1918 the timetable was left unaltered, except for minor timing changes, continuing right through to the 1940s. During the Second World War there was a substantial increase in freight traffic but this benefited the Banbury–Buckingham line and unfortunately this wartime traffic overlooked the N&BJR, limiting its ability to generate much needed revenue for the line.

Following nationalisation in 1948 the economic activity on both of these Banbury branch lines was diminishing and passenger numbers continued to fall. The N&BJR became the first casualty as passenger services between Banbury and Blisworth were withdrawn on 30th June 1951 with the last train consisting of a single coach hauled by a class 4F 0-6-0, No 44204.

Also running at a loss, the Banbury–Buckingham line actually fared better since measures were taken in 1956 to improve the situation by introducing a diesel railcar service. These were new single car 'Lightweight' units, both of which were built at Derby Works, numbered M79900 and M79901. The new service commenced from Banbury on 13th August 1956 with the 7.08 am departure to Bletchley.

Within four years the branch line was under threat of closure again. Although the operating loss had been reduced considerably, a loss had been made year on year and with this in mind and promises of a replacement bus service being provided by the Midland Red Omnibus Co, the line was scheduled for closure. On New Year's Eve 1960 the last train departed Banbury Merton Street for Buckingham, official closure to passengers being 2nd January 1961. Freight traffic continued until final closure came on 6th June 1966.

The third and final connection with the GWR at Banbury was the Great Central Railway (GCR) but in contrast to the above it

This is a picture of Banbury Merton Street station taken on 11th June 1961, five months after closure to passengers. It remained open for goods traffic until 6th June 1966 but downgraded to a coal depot only from 4th May 1964. An interesting assembly of vans and hopper wagons take refuge under a roofless canopy! (Author's Collection)

Most of the locomotives working the local services over the Great Central branch line from Culworth Junction to Banbury were allocated to Woodford Halse shed. This picture, full of atmosphere, was taken in 1965 with 'V2' class 2-6-2 No 60929 standing in the yard. (F.W. Shuttleworth)

had the blessing of the GWR! Following the GCR's successful London Extension in 1899 the two railways joined forces thereafter for their mutual benefit, particularly the GWR who had grand plans to improve its London–Birmingham timings.

For Banbury, however, the GWR encouraged the Great Central to build a branch line from Woodford Halse, the hub of operations for the London Extension, to Banbury where freight interchange facilities would be created. The 8½-mile double-track line, financed by the GWR, left the GCR's main line at Culworth Junction just south of Woodford Halse. It had two intermediate halts, Eydon Road and Chalcombe Road, and opened to freight traffic on 1st June 1900, followed by passenger services on 13th August.

The 'branch' line soon became part of an east–west cross-country corridor with Banbury at its centre. During the Second World War the line handled huge volumes of freight traffic and in 1940 more than 700,000 wagonloads were processed at the GCR's Banbury exchange yard.

Long-distance cross-country express services also became a feature of the line and when routed via the Banbury & Cheltenham Direct Railway, premier named trains such as the

A photograph showing the rebuilt Banbury station taken on 23rd April 1962. Standing at the platform, at the head of a passenger train is ex-GWR 'Modified Hall' class 4-6-0 No 7904 'Fowey Hall'. (Jeff Wood/Kidderminster Railway Museum)

Banbury shed played host to all manner of locomotives from Great Western 'Kings' to LNER 'V2s' and in British Railways' days various 'Standard' types such as this 'Britannia' class 4-6-0 No 70045, 'Lord Rowallan', standing over the ash pit waiting its next turn of duty, 13th November 1965. (Author's Collection)

This picture, taken around 1960, shows Banbury signal box situated at the end of the LNWR line from Verney Junction. It is an LMS type 11b box of brick and timber construction with gabled roof and stovepipe chimney with the stairway exiting at the far end. The operating room windows are of Design C and there are 4 brick-arched locking room windows. (D.A.N. Ratcliffe/Kidderminster Railway Museum)

Newcastle-upon-Tyne to Cardiff 'Ports to Ports Express' commenced operation. Other express passenger trains using the GCR line were Newcastle-upon-Tyne to Southampton, a York to Swindon sleeper service and Newcastle-upon-Tyne to Bournemouth.

Following nationalisation and despite the freight interchange sidings at Banbury being the busiest on the Western Region, economy measures were being planned and with the direct line from Banbury to Cheltenham closing in 1962 the capacity for cross-country express services was removed and the GCR branch line was looked upon as just a duplicate route to London.

Together with most of the Great Central lines in the area, the line closed on 5th September 1966 and although the GCR's exchange yard in Banbury continued operation, it too became a victim of BR's good housekeeping, closing on 4th October 1971.

Today very little remains of the 'foreign' railways that once connected with Banbury. On the Buckingham line from Verney Junction the trackbed to Banbury has more or less survived but walking the route, where only crumbling platforms and the odd culvert remain, may discourage all but the most determined railway enthusiast. However, the old station house at Fulwell & Westbury has survived and is in private ownership. At Cockley Brake Junction the area is completely overgrown and there is no trace of Farthinghoe station. At Banbury Merton Street there are no clues that a railway station existed here at all. The route of the GCR line can be found at Chacombe and north of Thorpe Mandeville. The N&BJR route has fared a little better and long stretches of the trackbed can be followed on foot. However, as the years pass by, these remnants, such as they are, become further hidden by nature.

One of the aspirations of the N&BJR was the conveyance of large quantities of iron ore from the Northamptonshire iron fields. But iron ore was also found in Oxfordshire, particularly

An interesting picture taken at Banbury of a very special train, reporting code 8X96, consisting of hauling engine BR class 5MT 4-6-0 No 73073, runner wagon, ex-LNER 'A3' 4-6-2 No 60008 'Dwight D. Eisenhower' and brake van. The date was Thursday 28th April 1964 and the ensemble was travelling from Doncaster to Southampton for 'presentation and shipment to the USA' where it was to become a museum exhibit. (F.W. Shuttleworth)

This picture, taken around 1960, shows the first station on the Great Central line from Banbury Junction to Woodford Halse. It is the diminutive Chalcombe Road Halt, near to the village of Chacombe and for whatever reason the Great Central added an 'l' to its name! (Author's Collection)

around the Banbury area, and this was usually referred to as the 'Oxfordshire Field'. The development of the Oxfordshire Field came with the opening of the Banbury–Cheltenham Direct line in 1887 when large deposits of ore were discovered at Hook Norton, and at Adderbury and Bloxham earlier-worked deposits were reopened.

The major part of the Oxfordshire Field lay in the Wroxton area just north of Banbury where the mining companies, realising the potential, took steps to build their own standard gauge railway to connect with the GWR's Oxford–Birmingham line.

No ironworks were built in the Oxfordshire Field apart from an experimental one at Adderbury, all the ore being sent away, mostly to Staffordshire and some to South Wales. The quarries were, in fact, entirely rural and the area was relatively untouched by the blot of heavy industry apart from the use of a few calcining kilns to render the ore.

Haulage on the tramways was undertaken by cable, steam locomotive and internal combustion locomotive, all rattling along on the prevalent 2′ gauge track, unlike the 3′ gauge, which at that time was by and large the standard for ironstone railways in other parts of the country.

The Oxfordshire Ironstone Co Ltd had the largest standard gauge ironstone tramway in the Midlands other than Corby whereas the Hook Norton Ironstone Co, which became Brymbo Steel Co Ltd from 1901, was the largest and most successful of the quarrying systems at Hook Norton and commenced operations in 1896 with a 2′ gauge tramway running from the quarries to two calcining kilns close to the south side of the GWR line. The first workings lay south of the railway but on the closure of the Partnership Quarries some of the leases for ground north of the GWR line, then known as Redland quarry, became the company's most productive quarrying area. The tramway to it passed beneath the GWR via an existing girder bridge where the original line ran roughly north-west from the bridge, turning northwards and then dividing. During the final years of operation the original pattern of track was replaced by a direct line that ran across the reclaimed ground to reach more remote but fertile workings.

Following extraction, some of the ore was calcined and then loaded via a chute into railway wagons standing on sidings at the rear of the kilns. Calcining was discontinued in 1926 but the kilns were left standing. However, the bulk of the iron ore output continued to go to Brymbo's Wrexham ironworks, transferred from narrow gauge tubs to standard railway wagons via tipplers set above the standard gauge siding. It was also the largest of the 2′ gauge systems in the ironstone industry and Hook Norton at that time was no doubt an interesting place, particularly with the chance of catching sight of the famous *Russell*, a 2-6-2T locomotive of the Welsh Highland Railway. When the WHR closed on 21st June 1937, *Russell* was left in the shed at Dinas Junction. As the threat of war loomed in Europe the closed line must have become an appealing source of scrap metal to seize for the war effort and the locomotive could easily have succumbed to the cutter's torch. Fortunately, *Russell* was purchased by the Brymbo Steel Co Ltd for use at Hook Norton alongside the resident 0-4-2 saddle tanks *Gwen* and *Joan* and 0-4-0ST *Betty*. The engine was overhauled at Brymbo's Wrexham Works and repainted to grey with black lining, in keeping with their two Hudswell Clarke locos.

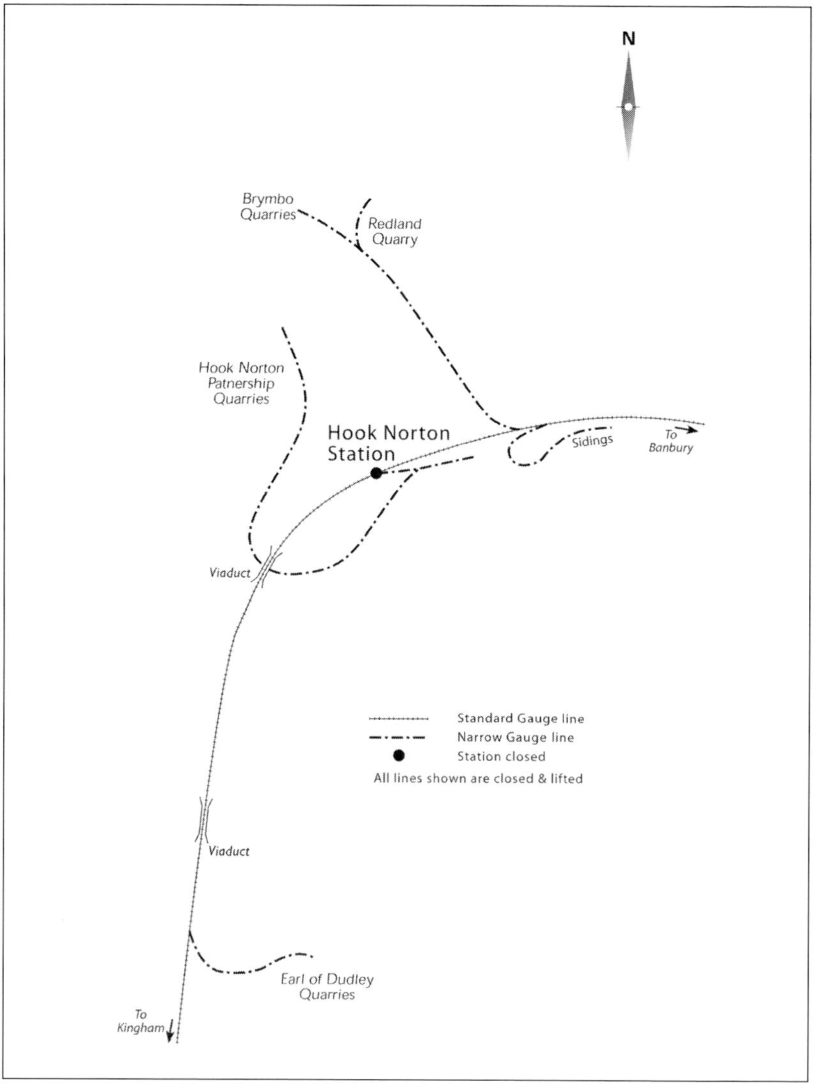

Russell was a powerful and capable locomotive but she was not designed for such sharp curves and uneven track and in order to reduce the frequent derailments, the leading pony truck was removed, but to no avail. During the Second World War the Hook Norton system reached its peak of production but the reduction in post-war business led to closure of the line in June

A photograph showing one of the Hook Norton Ironstone 1′ 11½″ gauge locomotives 'Russell', a 1906-built Hunslet 2-6-2T, at work on a train for the Brymbo Steel Co at Hook Norton mines on 22nd July 1943. (L.W. Perkins/W. Wycherley/Kidderminster Railway Museum)

This is a view of Hudswell Clarke 1′ 11½″ gauge 0-4-2ST 'Joan' shunting a Brymbo Steel Co's train at the calcining ovens of the Hook Norton Ironstone mines, 22nd July 1943. (L.W. Perkins/W. Wycherley/Kidderminster Railway Museum)

1946. *Russell* was relocated to Andover where she was eventually purchased by B. Fayle & Co Ltd, who worked the tramway at Corfe Castle. *Russell* was finally withdrawn from service in 1953 but was saved by the Birmingham Locomotive Club, who bought the engine and transported her to the Talyllyn Railway Preservation Society.

As indicated above, the largest of the Oxfordshire ironstone fields was situated in the Wroxton area. In 1917 a new company was formed, the Oxfordshire Ironstone Co Ltd, comprising Stewarts & Lloyds Ltd, Baldwins Ltd and Brymbo Steel Co Ltd. Construction of the standard gauge line began in the autumn of 1917 with ore extraction starting in 1919.

One-and-a-quarter miles north of Banbury station a junction was made with the Oxford–Birmingham main line where substantial transfer sidings were provided and the web of lines to the junction was controlled by the 'Ironstone Mines signal box'. This was the start of the five miles of 'main line' – mostly double track – that ran through undulating and pleasing countryside. When the line was constructed it was looked upon as one of the finest ironstone tramways in the country. It was anticipated that the intense activity on the line warranted a

A picture of Hudswell Clarke 1' 11½" gauge 0-4-2ST 'Gwen' at Hook Norton Ironstone mines, about to pass beneath the bridge carrying the Banbury–Kingham line, heading a train of tubs back to the exchange sidings. (L.W. Perkins/W. Wycherley/Kidderminster Railway Museum)

On 25th August 1946 standard gauge Hudswell Clarke 0-6-0T 'Lord North' stands in the yard of Oxfordshire Ironstone Co Ltd at Wroxton, seen partly dismantled for major overhaul. (L.W. Perkins/W. Wycherley/Kidderminster Railway Museum)

railway of this standard, which featured signal boxes, crossing gates and a telegraph system.

Starting from the junction the line headed south-west over the A423 Southam–Banbury road, passing additional sidings and calcining kilns. Turning west the line passed beneath the B4100, Warwick Road, before heading north-west to meet the first signal-box-controlled level crossing, protecting the Wroxton–Hanwell road. Turning west again the railway passed over a bridge spanning the Wroxton–Horley road before heading south to the main quarry sidings and the second signal-box-controlled level crossing, over the Wroxton–Hornton unclassified road. The locomotive sheds were situated at this point, together with coal and watering stages, and it was where the line divided as three single tracks to the quarries at Balscote, Langley and to the furthest extent of the railway, Horton Grounds, situated alongside the A422 Stratford upon Avon road.

From 1918 no fewer than 29 locomotives were acquired to work the system, mostly 0-4-0 and 0-6-0 tank engines purchased new from Hudswell Clarke, Peckett or Hunslet. They were maintained and allocated from the sheds at Wroxton, operating

This is an undated view of an immaculate Hunslet standard gauge 0-6-0ST 'Graham', works No 2415, of 1941, as it stands by the shed at the Oxfordshire Ironstone Co Ltd, Wroxton complex. A roster board attached to the side of the building indicates that it is a Monday and this particular locomotive is not listed for duty. (J. Tarrant/Kidderminster Railway Museum)

On 23rd April 1960 Oxfordshire Ironstone Co Ltd standard gauge locomotive Hudswell Clarke 0-4-0ST No 6, 'Gwen', shunts tippler wagons at Wroxton. (L.W. Perkins/W. Wycherley/Kidderminster Railway Museum)

This is part of the former Oxfordshire Ironstone Co Ltd, Wroxton complex, in July 2009, following removal of the engine shed and workshops. Beyond the gate the trackbed is still in situ. The loco shed and workshops would have taken up the area on the right of the picture. (Author)

Viewed from the opposite direction to the above picture in July 2009, the main Wroxton site is now occupied by the Apollo Office Park and sadly the area gives no indication at all to its industrial railway heritage. (Author)

without interruption until the downturn in demand for iron ore brought about the line's closure in 1965, with the whole system closing down in September 1967.

There are still some reminders of the ironstone lines around the Wroxton area and these sites are recorded by Oxfordshire County Council. Langley Quarry is listed as an 'Ironstone Pit and Railway Siding' at grid reference: SP391432. Similarly, the remains of the railway from Wroxton is listed as a 'linear feature' and 'Railway Branch between Wroxton and Just N of Banbury'. The main site at Wroxton is listed as 'Wroxton Ironstone Works and Site of Ironstone Quarry' and 'Quarry and Locomotive depot'. Features of the railway are still visible along the former route and although the road bridges have been taken out, abutments remain to give witness to its railway past. At Wroxton, the most tangible evidence, in the form of a locomotive shed, workshops and offices, stood intact until 2005 when the developers of the Apollo Office Park were granted planning consent to develop the main site to accommodate a number of small high-end units, such as the Bentley Owners Club. Unfortunately, the locomotive shed and workshops, which should have been protected monuments to this once thriving industry, were demolished prior to the tenants taking possession. I enquired about this and a local man said that he had asked someone whom he believed to be one of the contractors why the old railway buildings were being dismantled and was told: 'So that no one can come along and put a preservation order on them.'

At Hook Norton, locations and features of the three main ironstone works are listed as (1) 'Ironstone Quarries, Railway Sidings (Hook Norton Quarries Partnership)', grid reference: SP362338; (2) 'Ironstone Quarries, Railway sidings and Kilns (Hook Norton Earl of Dudley's Quarries)', grid reference: SP362325; (3) 'Ironstone Quarries, Railway sidings and Kilns (Hook Norton Quarries, Brymbo and Redlands)', grid reference: SP3634.

So there we have it, three railways connecting with Banbury that ran for the most part outside Oxfordshire but between them shaped a junction station of great consequence – and when closure came they were indeed railways lost to Oxfordshire.

Closure of the ironstone lines, wholly within Oxfordshire, had a significant bearing on the community because of the social and economic impact following the closure of the ironstone works and the consequential loss of the railways that supported it.

12
The Didcot, Newbury & Southampton Railway

A picture of the turntable at Didcot shed with visiting locomotive ex-Southern Railway 'T9' class 4-4-0 No 30288 of Eastleigh (71a) shed being turned for its next duty, 19th June 1956. (Author's Collection)

In reality, the Didcot, Newbury & Southampton Railway (DN&SR) was never part of Oxfordshire, either in conception or during its demise, but Parliamentary boundary changes introduced in 1974 brought Didcot and part of the former railway's alignment within the county of Oxfordshire. Nevertheless, as a conclusion to this volume, I have included a brief account of this interesting railway, which made it to Southampton in the face of relentless opposition and during the two world wars became one of the most strategically important lines in the country.

A settlement has existed at Didcot since the Iron Age and because of its elevated position it was also an area of Roman

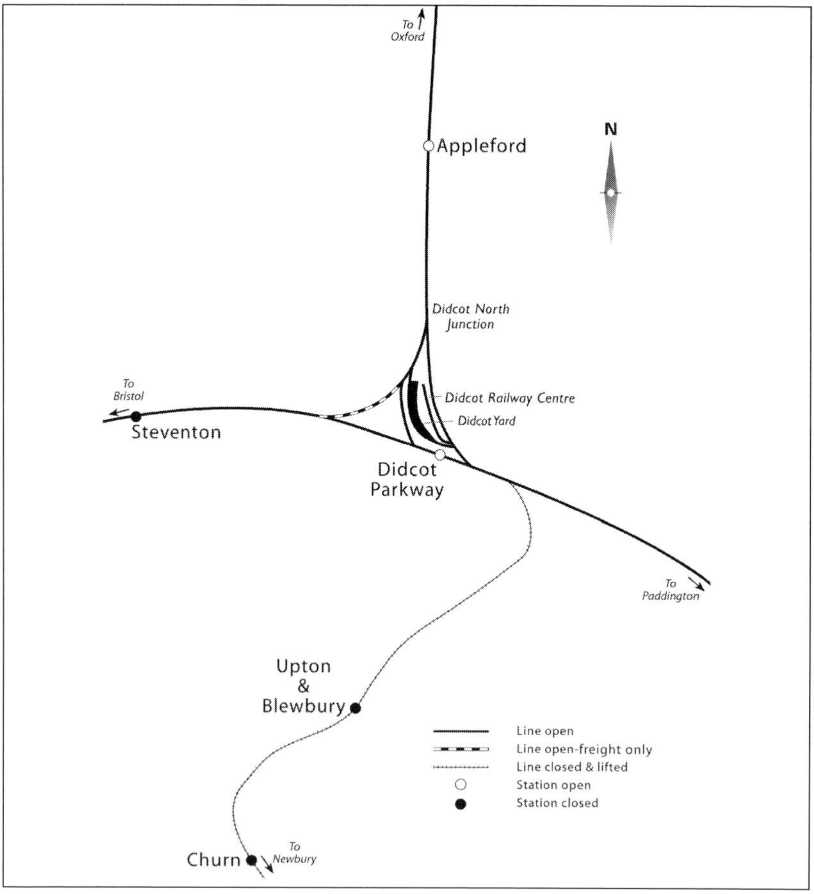

occupation. Part of All Saints' church dates back to the 11th century but the earliest records, naming the village as *Dudcotte*, appeared in the 13th century.

For the next 600 years or so, the village remained as a sleepy Berkshire hamlet until the arrival of Brunel's Great Western Railway from Paddington to Bristol. On 1st June 1840 the section from Reading to Steventon opened; a new station was provided at the latter and as the nearest station to Didcot (at 4 miles distant) it was not exactly convenient for the townspeople. It would have remained this way had it not been for the residents of Abingdon who objected to a proposed line from Steventon to Oxford, with Abingdon as its intermediate station. Their intervention eventually led to the Oxford Railway being opened in 1844 (see Chapter 1), this time from a junction at Didcot where Brunel built a grand 'Paddington' style wooden train shed and so established Didcot's place in railway history.

During the mid-1840s a number of schemes were promoted to provide a direct route from the north of England to the south coast, all of which would be required to traverse the GWR's broad gauge London–Bristol main line at or near Didcot.

One of these schemes, promoted by the Manchester & Southampton Railway (M&SR), almost succeeded in obtaining approval for a standard gauge line that would have created a junction to negotiate the broad gauge line at Didcot. Vigorous opposition, however, from the GWR thwarted this project and Parliament voted against it.

Twenty-five years went by before promoters took steps to reawaken a similar scheme, and during this time the London & South Western Railway (LSWR) had been busy south of Didcot, building a standard gauge main line from Salisbury, Andover and Basingstoke, whilst the GWR had laid mixed gauge track from Oxford to join with the LSWR at Basingstoke. This left the hinterland between Didcot and Newbury without access to a rapidly expanding railway network and, more importantly, mounting pressure from industrialists who were anxious to move coal supplies (amongst other things) from South Wales to major ports, such as Southampton, to fuel increasing numbers of steam-powered vessels.

By 1872, even though much of the GWR's broad gauge had been converted to standard gauge or mixed gauge, goods traffic from the north or coal trains from South Wales were still required to negotiate a long and tedious route to reach Southampton.

The following year, on 5th August 1873, an Act of Parliament incorporated the Didcot, Newbury & Southampton Junction Railway (the 'Junction' later being dropped) authorising a railway to be built, 34 miles in length, from a junction east of Didcot station to a junction with the LSWR near Micheldever.

It was to be another six years before the necessary finance was accrued to build the line. The appointment of railway engineer John Fowler and contractors Sir Thomas Tancred and T.H. Falkiner was agreed on 9th August 1879, followed by the first 'sod' being cut by Lady Carnarvon on 26th August 1879 during an uninspiring ceremony at a site near London Road, Newbury.

Construction started the following year and work progressed on the line at a rapid pace, including the provision of four intermediate stations, resulting in the line being ready for its formal opening on 12th April 1882. An agreement had been made with the GWR to operate services on behalf of the DN&SR and a public service commenced the following day with five return trains timetabled each weekday (Monday to Saturday) between Newbury and Didcot, the company directors announcing at the time 'about 50 villages are thus accommodated'. Motive power for the northern section was provided by the Great Western's Didcot shed and would have probably been one of Armstrong's 0-6-0 saddle tanks or a Metropolitan 2-4-0 tank engine.

South of Newbury, however, there was a range of inter-company territorial problems arising that would ultimately delay progress of the DN&SR towards Southampton, particularly the growing hostility between the GWR and LSWR. By this time the DN&SR had obtained powers, much to the annoyance of the GWR and LSWR, to build its southern extension to Southampton and establish a terminus station.

This competition was not welcome and ironically it culminated in a peace treaty between the GWR and LSWR. Notwithstanding this the DN&SR pushed ahead and the section of line, between Newbury and a terminus station in Winchester, was finally opened on 1st May 1885, followed by the public service starting on 4th May 1885. Now, to complete the railway to Southampton required substantial capital that the DN&SR did not possess and was not likely to obtain from private investors.

A positive outcome emerged in October 1889 when the three companies formed a joint agreement in which the DN&SR would not proceed with a competing line to Southampton in return for a working arrangement where Great Western trains would work DN&SR services from the north into Winchester and locomotives would be changed here for LSWR motive power to carry the train forward over the existing lines to Southampton.

The agreement, however, required a new line of 1½ miles to connect with a new junction at Shawford. The cost of this work was met partly by the DN&SR, reclaiming its Parliamentary deposits for lines it no longer wished to develop, and a generous loan from the LSWR.

On 1st October 1891 the Shawford Junction line, as it was

called, opened to traffic and finally it was possible for through trains to run between Didcot and Southampton, albeit with a locomotive change at Winchester. This practice continued for almost 20 years when pooling arrangements between the DN&SR and LSWR resulted in some Great Western engines working through to Southampton Docks station.

The pattern of passenger services seems to have been established, at four return trains each weekday (Monday to Saturday), as the line opened to Winchester and a similar timetable continued when the line was extended to Southampton.

As with many branch lines in Britain, the First World War affected the DN&SR passenger services to a point where they were suspended between Didcot and Winchester to make way for numerous military movements. During the conflict the railway proved its potential for north–south freight traffic as trains from various quarters, including coal trains from the Leicestershire coalfields, operated over the DN&SR.

Following absorption by the GWR during the grouping in 1923, very little changed on the railway. The passenger timetable consisted of four return trains each weekday between Didcot and Southampton, with morning and afternoon 'locals' running between Newbury and Didcot and Newbury and Winchester.

The line's strategic importance became clear during the Second World War when it was decided to introduce double track from Didcot Junction to Newbury. Work started in October 1942 and was completed by 8th March 1943, when passenger services recommenced. The doubling of the line and associated works cannot be undervalued as it was carried out in preparation for the D-Day landings on 6th June 1944 to supply the vast quantities of weapons, ammunition, troops and supporting equipment from Didcot, where extensive Army and RAF ordnance depots had been built, to transit areas established near Southampton. Although no official figures appear to be available it seems that during a 13-month period prior to the Normandy Campaign the number of military trains using the line exceeded 16,000!

As the war ended, though, the long period of closure took its toll on future patronage since passengers had found other modes of travel and most remained with their individual choice. But the railway continued, returning to a sleepy country branch line with stations such as Upton & Blewbury and Churn (the

This picture of a very well-kept Upton & Blewbury station, taken in 1961, shows all the station's attributes, consisting of main station building, the opposite platform with waiting shelter and a signal box. (E.T. Gill/ R.K. Blencowe Archive)

sites of which now reside in Oxfordshire) that would regularly witness the passage of an ex-GWR 2-4-0 tank engine and two coaches of diverse vintage ambling along with a summer evening train to Newbury.

Churn station consisted of a long island platform, which was adapted to accommodate troop trains, and during its twilight years as passenger numbers were decreasing, the timetable had an interesting footnote which stated that trains would stop to take up/set down passengers on prior notice to the Didcot stationmaster, adding a cautionary note, 'Evening trains call during daylight only'!

As passenger numbers diminished, the threat of closure came with the Beeching Report and on 10th September 1962 Churn and Upton & Blewbury stations closed to passengers. Freight traffic continued until 19th May 1964 when Upton & Blewbury was demoted to 'Coal Depot' only, followed by final closure, along with the rest of the line, taking place on 10th August 1964. Churn had already lost its goods facility when the freight siding was lifted on 14th April 1943.

A picture of Churn station c1962, showing the island platform created and lengthened during the Second World War to take troop trains. It looks wonderfully isolated with its single brick shelter, which begs the question – how did it attract passengers? (Lens of Sutton Collection)

Didcot Motive Power depot closed in June 1965 with most of its allocation being transferred to Oxford shed. Two years later the Didcot shed and sidings were occupied by the Great Western Society to create what is now known as the Didcot Railway Centre. It is accessed through Didcot station and provides the visitor with an extensive collection of preserved steam locomotives, passenger stock and a number of original structures and various railway artefacts.

Didcot station was renamed Didcot Parkway on 29th July 1985, signifying its role as a Park & Ride station. It has five platforms to serve trains for London, Cardiff, Swansea, Oxford, Hereford and the north. Didcot is still a major junction and marshalling yard but the significant Army and RAF ordnance depots, referred to earlier, have succumbed to the ravages of development and lie somewhere beneath Didcot Power Station.

The closure of the DN&SR could well have been a missed opportunity since it was intended primarily as a direct route from the industrial West Midlands and the north to the south coast ports and had it been available today it would have provided a compelling alternative to the hundreds of juggernauts that trundle relentlessly along the M40 and A34.

But then, it would not be a lost railway.

Bibliography

Whilst compiling *Lost Railways of Oxfordshire* I have referred to various contemporary documents, timetables, newspapers and numerous Ordnance Survey maps. I found several 1950s' copies of *The Railway Magazine* very helpful in confirming items of detail. The following publications have also been consulted and although some of these are now out of print they are well worth seeking out to provide a more detailed read:

Baker, S.K. *Rail Atlas of Great Britain & Ireland, 3rd and 11th editions* (OPC)
Christiansen, Rex *A Regional History of the Railways of Great Britain, vol 13, Thames & Severn* (David & Charles)
Clinker, C.R. *Clinker's Register of Closed Passenger Stations and Goods Depots 1830–1977* (Avon Anglia Publications)
Cockman, F.G. *Discovering Lost Railways* (Shire Publications Ltd)
Connolly, W. Philip *British Railways Pre-Grouping Atlas & Gazetteer, 5th edition* (Ian Allan)
Daniels, Gerald & Dench, *Les Passengers No More* (Ian Allan)
Green, Martin *Railway Walks – Gloucestershire, Wiltshire and Oxfordshire* (Rearden Publishing)
Jenkins, Stanley C. *The Witney & East Gloucestershire Railway* (Fairford Branch) (The Oakwood Press)
Jenkins, Stanley C. *The Northampton & Banbury Junction Railway* (The Oakwood Press)
Healy, John M.C. *Great Central Memories* (Baton Transport)
Karau, Paul & Turner, Chris *The Wallingford Branch* (Wild Swan Publications)
Lingard, Richard *The Woodstock Branch* (Oxford Publishing Co)
Lingard, Richard *Princes Risborough–Thame–Oxford Railway* (Oxford Publishing Co)
Phillips, Daphne *How the Great Western Came to Berkshire: a Railway History 1832–1882* (Reading Libraries)
Robertson, Kevin *The Last Days of Steam in Oxfordshire* (Alan Sutton)
Russell, J.H. *The Banbury and Cheltenham Railway 1887–1962* (Oxford Publishing Co)
Sands, T.B. *The Didcot, Newbury & Southampton Railway* (The Oakwood Press)
Searle, Muriel V. *Lost Lines: An Anthology of Britain's Lost Railways* (New Cavendish Books)
Simpson, Bill *The Banbury to Verney Junction Branch* (Oxford Publishing Co)
Tonks, Eric S. *The Ironstone Railways and Tramways of the Midlands* (Locomotive Publishing Co Ltd)
Vaughan, Adrian *A History of The Faringdon Branch and Uffington Station* (Oxford Publishing Co)
Waters, Laurence *Rail Centres: Oxford* (Ian Allan)
Wilkinson, Reg *The Wantage Tramway* (The Oakwood Press)
Woodcock, George *Minor Railways of England and their Locomotives* (Goose & Son Publishers)

INDEX